TIME ZONES

WORKBOOK | THIRD EDITION

DAVID BOHLKE

NATIONAL GEOGRAPHIC
LEARNING

Australia · Brazil · Mexico · Singapore · United Kingdom · United States

National Geographic Learning,
a Cengage Company

Time Zones Workbook 4 Third Edition
David Bohlke

Publisher: Andrew Robinson

Managing Editor: Derek Mackrell

Associate Development Editor: Yvonne Tan

Additional Editorial Support: Sarah Jane Lewis

Director of Global Marketing: Ian Martin

Senior Product Marketing Manager: Anders Bylund

Heads of Regional Marketing:
  Charlotte Ellis (Europe, Middle East and Africa)
  Irina Pereyra (Latin America)

Senior Production Controller: Tan Jin Hock

Associate Media Researcher: Jeffrey Millies

Senior Designer: Lisa Trager

Operations Support: Rebecca G. Barbush,
  Hayley Chwazik-Gee

Manufacturing Planner: Mary Beth Hennebury

Composition: Symmetry Creative Production, Inc.

For permission to use material from this text or product, submit all requests online at **cengage.com/permissions**
Further permissions questions can be emailed to **permissionrequest@cengage.com**

ISBN-13: 978-0-357-42636-4

National Geographic Learning
200 Pier 4 Boulevard
Boston, MA 02210
USA

Locate your local office at **international.cengage.com/region**

Visit National Geographic Learning online at **ELTNGL.com**
Visit our corporate website at **www.cengage.com**

Printed in the United States of America
Print Number: 07 Print Year: 2024

CONTENTS

1

I LOVE MIXING MUSIC!

PREVIEW

A **Match.** Where would you do these activities? Match the activities with the places.

1 swimming ○   ○ **a** on a mountain

2 skiing ○   ○ **b** in a kitchen

3 cooking ○   ○ **c** in a pool

4 exercising ○   ○ **d** in a gym

B **Complete the sentences.** Use the words and phrases in the box.

> cooking   dancing   ~~drawing~~   gardening
> Instagramming   making videos   ~~mixing music~~   reading comic books

1 Aaron loves getting his pen and paper out and creating new superheroes. He also enjoys using the GarageBand app to combine different song tracks.

Aaron loves _____ *drawing and mixing music* _____.

2 Megan likes planting and taking care of flowers in her backyard. She sometimes posts photos of the flowers on her favorite social networking site.

Megan likes _____.

3 Layla enjoys turning up the music in her bedroom and practicing her dance moves. She also enjoys reading stories about superheroes such as *Batman* and *X-Men*.

Layla enjoys _____.

4 Pedro likes trying out new recipes in the kitchen. He sometimes films himself in the kitchen and then posts the video on YouTube.

Pedro likes _____ .

C **Write.** Name one of your hobbies. Where and when do you do it?

_____

LANGUAGE FOCUS

A **Correct the error in each sentence.**

1 I don't like dancing, but I enjoy sing.

2 Read fantasy books is fun, but I like reading graphic novels more.

3 Jan likes cooking, but she doesn't enjoy to bake at all.

4 I don't like watching movies on my iPad. I like see them in a theater.

5 I don't like doing puzzles. In fact, I wouldn't stand it.

B **Unscramble the words to form questions.** Then complete the answers.

1 **A:** (*Mike / like / does / playing golf*) Does Mike like playing golf _____ ?

B: No, he can't _____stand_____ it.

2 **A:** (*what / doing / Hal and Linda / do / enjoy*) _____ ?

B: They enjoy _____ jigsaw puzzles.

3 **A:** (*cooking / like / do / you*) _____ ?

B: No, I don't really _____ cooking.

4 **A:** (*Charles / like / does / doing / what*) _____ ?

B: He likes _____ video games.

C **Complete the conversation.** Put the sentences in the correct order (1–7).

a __1__ I'm bored. Do you feel like doing something?

b _____ Great! I love playing video games, but I'm not very good at it.

c _____ I love it, but I think it might rain later. Maybe we can bake cookies instead?

d _____ Sure. What would you like to do?

e _____ Baking cookies doesn't sound very fun, sorry. What about a video game?

f _____ Well, do you like hiking?

g _____ That's OK. I'm not, either.

LEISURE TIME **SURVEY**

A Skim the article. The article compares leisure activities _____.

a in different countries   **b** between boys and girls   **c** between two age groups

Leisure time is important for everyone. But what do people actually enjoy doing in their free time? The U.S. Bureau of Labor Statistics conducted a survey to ask millennials (people born between 1981 and 2000) and retirees (people older than 65 years) this question. The graph below shows that when it comes to free time, the two groups don't have much in common.

One big difference between these two groups is the amount of reading they do. Millennials spend very little time reading compared to retirees. Retirees also spend twice as much time as millennials watching TV. On the whole, the survey found that retirees fill their time with activities to keep themselves occupied, whereas millennials use their free time to relax.

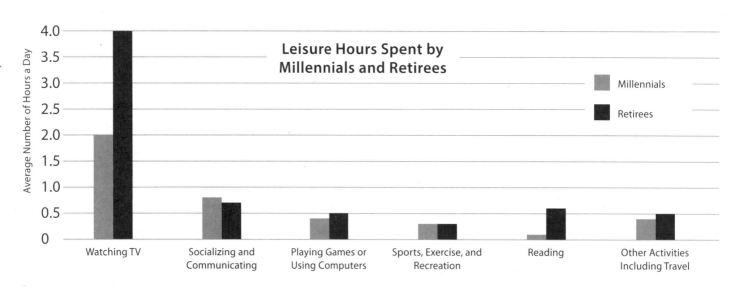

B **Read the article and look at the graph.** Circle **T** for true or **F** for false.

1 Retirees are people who have stopped working. **T F**

2 Millennials spend about four hours of their leisure time watching TV. **T F**

3 Both groups spend fewer than 30 minutes every day on socializing. **T F**

4 Millennials spend more of their leisure time on sports than retirees. **T F**

5 Millennials have fewer hours of free time than retirees. **T F**

READING

A **Scan the article.** Underline the six hobbies mentioned.

WHAT'S OLD IS NEW AGAIN

Put down that phone! More and more young people today are beginning to tire of technology, and have been turning to the hobbies of their parents—and even grandparents! It seems that what was once old-fashioned is now hip. Millennials have found a new interest in making things with their own hands. This DIY culture has resulted
5 in hobbies that are cheap, don't require a lot of space, and are easy to do!

Canning, soap making, and beekeeping have become more popular in recent years. Canning is a way of making food last longer. It's a great way to prepare homemade jams, jellies, and pickles for family and friends. Soap making is for people who like to make soap that is healthy for the skin and doesn't contain harmful chemicals. And beekeeping has
10 many benefits besides providing honey. Beeswax can be used to make candles, lip gloss, and wood polish.

Other DIY hobbies include baking, embroidery, and writing. With the success of TV shows like *The Great British Baking Show* and *Cake Wars*, baking is more popular than ever. Embroidery is a craft that involves
15 decorating fabrics by hand using a needle and thread. Those who enjoy embroidery often decorate pillows or sew inspirational sayings onto fabric, which they then hang on a wall. And writing in the DIY sense refers to writing letters and journals using a pen and paper or an old typewriter, instead of using a computer.

20 For some millennials, this DIY culture is a way to set themselves apart. For others, it's a good way to save money. But perhaps what appeals most to millennials is the sense of achievement they get from these DIY hobbies.

Embroidery is growing in popularity.

B **Answer the questions about *What's Old Is New Again*.**

1 GIST What could be another title for the article?

   a The Joys of Canning   **b** Millennials' Hobbies   **c** Making Time for Hobbies

2 VOCABULARY The word *hip* in line 3 can be replaced with _____ .

   a outdated   **b** trendy   **c** fancy

3 **INFERENCE** *DIY* probably stands for _____ .

    a doing it young   **b** do it yearly   **c** do it yourself

4 **DETAIL** According to the article, DIY hobbies _____ .

    a cost a lot of money   **b** are becoming less popular   **c** can be fulfilling

5 **INFERENCE** Which of the following hobbies is NOT similar to the ones mentioned in the article?

    a playing soccer   **b** knitting   **c** making furniture

C **EXAM PRACTICE** **Match the hobbies with the descriptions given in the article.**

1 Canning   ○   ○ **a** creates something you can frame and hang on the wall.

2 Soap making   ○   ○ **b** creates something used in making candles.

3 Beekeeping   ○   ○ **c** may involve using paper and an old machine.

4 Baking   ○   ○ **d** is a way to make fruits and vegetables last longer.

5 Embroidery   ○   ○ **e** is shown on popular TV shows.

6 Writing   ○   ○ **f** creates something that is good for your skin.

VOCABULARY

A **Complete the sentences.** Use the words in the box.

> affect   appear   average   eventually   leader   post

1 I'm going to _____ on a TV show tomorrow to talk about our school.

2 I hope my project on the environment will _____ people's attitudes toward recycling.

3 It took some time, but Keiko _____ finished her embroidery project.

4 The _____ age of players on our mother–daughter soccer team is 28.

5 I often read online comments, but I rarely _____ my own.

6 Who do you think would be a better _____ for the team: Ann or Lucas?

B **Complete the sentences.** Circle the correct answers.

1 Your opinion will have no **affect** / **effect** on how I feel.

2 The town **council** / **counsel** will hold its first meeting tomorrow.

3 I don't know what to do. Can you give me some **advice** / **advise**?

4 Teachers can **council** / **counsel** you on the best classes to take.

5 Do you think the new rule will **affect** / **effect** us negatively?

6 If the problem continues, what would you **advice** / **advise** me to do?

WRITING

CREATING AN OUTLINE

Use an outline to organize your ideas before you write. An outline shows main ideas and supporting details. As you begin writing, you can omit or add information.

> **OUTLINE**
>
> **What I Like Doing**
>
> Sports
>
> - watching soccer: favorite players, World Cup, ...
>
> - playing tennis: lessons, future goals, ...
>
> Watching movies
>
> - at the movie theater
>
> - at home: watch on TV, downloads, streaming, ...

A Read the passage below. Underline the information in the passage that also appears in the outline.

I have a very busy schedule at school, so I don't have a lot of free time. But when I do, I love watching soccer. Two of my favorite players are Kylian Mbappé and Mohamed Salah. I especially love watching World Cup matches. I play sports, too. I take tennis lessons twice a week and hope to be on the school team next year.

I also enjoy watching movies. I sometimes go to a theater to see a movie, but I like watching movies at home more. I like watching old movies on TV with my parents. When my friends come over, we usually stream movies on my computer.

B Plan an essay. Create an outline to answer this question: "What do the people in your family like doing?"

C Use your outline from B to write a short essay. You may choose to omit information from your outline or add new information.

HOW LONG HAVE **YOU BEEN DOING** ARCHERY?

PREVIEW

A Complete the crossword puzzle. Use the pictures to help you.

B Write. Which activities in **A** require a ball?

_____

LANGUAGE FOCUS

A **Correct the error in each sentence.**

1 Kevin has been studying since over an hour.

2 What have you been lately doing?

3 How long has you and your friends been waiting here?

4 Jessica has been work at the sports center since July.

B **Complete the questions and answers.** Use the correct form of the words in parentheses. Add *for* or *since* if necessary.

1 **A:** How long has Andy _____? (*go to the gym*)

   B: He _____ . (*two years*)

2 **A:** Has Ana _____?
     (*take tennis lessons / a long time*)

   B: Yes, she _____ .
     (*middle school*)

3 **A:** How long has _____? (*rain*)

   B: It _____ . (*about an hour*)

4 **A:** Have you _____? (*watch TV / long*)

   B: Yes, I _____ . (*8:30*)

C **Match.** Join the two parts of the conversation.

1 Hey, Karl! I haven't seen you in a while! What are you doing here? ◯

2 Why don't you try calling him? ◯

3 Yeah, he's probably on the way. So what are you guys going to do? ◯

4 Not much. I've been working here at Café Central for the last couple of months. I'm trying to save money for college. ◯

◯ a I did, but he's not answering his phone. I'll try and call him again if he's not here soon.

◯ b Oh, yeah? I have a part-time job, too. I've been tutoring kids in English since May.

◯ c Hi, Jan! How are you? I was supposed to meet Brian here. I guess he's running late.

◯ d We're going to watch a baseball game. The team we like has been playing well recently, so it should be a good game. Anyway, what's new with you?

A Headis player

HEADIS

A Scan the article. What two sports does Headis combine? _____ and _____

The game of Headis is played on a table tennis table, but instead of a paddle, players use their heads to hit a ball back and forth. The sport combines elements of table tennis and soccer. The ball is made of rubber and is bigger and heavier than a tennis ball. Only a player's head can touch the ball, but any part of their body can touch the table. Each game is played to 11 points.

The sport started in 2006 in Germany. A college student named René Wegner and his friends wanted to play a game of soccer, but the soccer field was being used. They found a table tennis table instead, and began hitting a rubber ball back and forth using just their heads. Headis's popularity grew quickly. Soon, Wegner's university made the new sport part of its sports program. That same year, Germany held its first countrywide competition.

More recently, people have been playing Headis in England, Spain, and France. There are now international competitions with an estimated 80,000 players. Interestingly, players don't use their real names in Headis. Instead, they choose names like Marvelous 96 or Headi Potter.

B Read the article. Choose the correct answers.

1 Headis players use a ball that is _____ a tennis ball.

   a smaller than   **b** bigger than   **c** the same size as

2 Headis players _____ touch the table with their body.

   a can   **b** can't   **c** must

3 What is the second paragraph mainly about?

   a how Headis is different from soccer

   b why René Wegner chose a table tennis table

   c the birth and growth of Headis

4 Which of these names would you probably NOT find in a Headis game?

    a Success 101   **b** Paddy O'Paddles   **c** John Peterson

READING

A **Skim the article.** The article is about Ramón Navarro's work as a surfer and _____ .

    a conservationist   **b** politician   **c** journalist

WAVES OF CHANGE

A "In my dreams, I'd never thought a wave could be that perfect," says Chilean surfer Ramón Navarro of the wave he surfed in Fiji in June 2012. The wave was a perfect, curling tube big enough to drive a truck through. He surfed it so beautifully that many surfers have called it the best tube ride ever.

B Navarro has been surfing since he was 12. He comes from a family of fishermen, which had a big influence on him. As a child, his parents taught him to care about the ocean; he says it was one of the first things he knew about. Today, he is one of the best big-wave surfers in the world.

Ramón Navarro

C Navarro is passionate about surfing, but he is also actively involved in protecting the ocean around his birthplace of Punta de Lobos. When he learned that a sewage pipe was going to release untreated waste into the bay of his hometown, he decided to do something about it. He reached out to local politicians and international organizations. He also organized surfers and locals to speak against the pipe project. His efforts successfully prevented water pollution in the area.

D Navarro has also been working with conservation groups and the Chilean government to turn the stretch of coast in his hometown into a national park. They work together to protect the area from industrial activities, such as the building of large dams. For the people of Chile, conservation is a way to bring in tourism. For Navarro, it's about protecting his own corner of the country.

E "The Chilean people have been really involved in the environmental movement," says Navarro. "If we protect our land, take care of our country, we will have a better standard of living."

B **Answer the questions about *Waves of Change*.**

    1 MAIN IDEA Navarro is working to get people to _____ .

        a take up surfing   **b** protect the ocean   **c** practice safe fishing techniques

    2 DETAIL Who taught Navarro to care about the ocean?

        a fellow surfers   **b** fishermen in Fiji   **c** his parents

3 VOCABULARY What's another word for *passionate* in paragraph C?

  a enthusiastic   **b** knowledgeable   **c** confident

4 DETAIL What did Navarro do to prevent water pollution in his hometown?

  a He created a website.

  b He built a special water filter.

  c He approached the government.

5 INFERENCE Who is most likely to object to Navarro's proposal for a national park?

  a local residents   **b** the Chilean government   **c** factory owners

C EXAM PRACTICE **Match each paragraph with its main topic.**

  1 Paragraph A ○   ○ **a** what got Navarro interested in the ocean as a child

  2 Paragraph B ○   ○ **b** how Navarro has been trying to establish a new national park

  3 Paragraph C ○   ○ **c** how Navarro surfed the perfect wave

  4 Paragraph D ○   ○ **d** what Chileans need to do to improve their lives

  5 Paragraph E ○   ○ **e** how Navarro helped protect the ocean from pollution

VOCABULARY

A **Complete the sentences.** Use the words in the box.

> announce   defeat   determination   distance   previous   success

  1 The _____ of our project depends on getting people to care.

  2 The runners covered the _____ in less than 30 minutes.

  3 Listen—they're about to _____ the winner of the race.

  4 The _____ game was much more exciting than this one.

  5 He says it was hard work and _____ that got him over the finish line.

  6 The tennis player was able to _____ her opponent in record time.

B **Complete the sentences.** Circle the correct answers.

  1 Who **holds** / **sets** the Olympic record for the long jump?

  2 The nurse updated my **financial** / **medical** records with my height and weight.

  3 We cleaned the house in **record time** / **permanent record**.

  4 I want to beat the **world** / **broken** record for the men's high jump.

  5 No one has been able to **set** / **break** his record in the 100-meter race.

WRITING

WRITING TIP **COMBINING SENTENCES**

To avoid too many short sentences and to make your writing more natural, combine sentences. You can join ideas together using words like **and**, **but**, **or**, and **so**.

> *I've been playing soccer for years, **and** I'm very good at it.*
> **(adding information)**
>
> *I like playing basketball, **but** I don't like playing baseball.*
> **(contrasting information)**
>
> *I may go to the game on Friday, **or** I may watch it on TV.*
> **(stating a choice)**
>
> *I have a tennis lesson tomorrow morning, **so** I can't stay out late.*
> **(stating a result)**

A **Read the email below.** Underline the combined sentences.

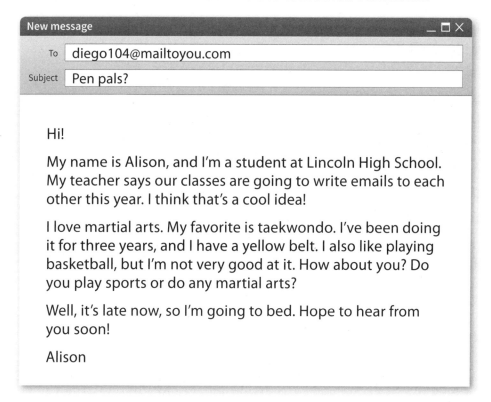

New message

To   diego104@mailtoyou.com

Subject   Pen pals?

Hi!

My name is Alison, and I'm a student at Lincoln High School. My teacher says our classes are going to write emails to each other this year. I think that's a cool idea!

I love martial arts. My favorite is taekwondo. I've been doing it for three years, and I have a yellow belt. I also like playing basketball, but I'm not very good at it. How about you? Do you play sports or do any martial arts?

Well, it's late now, so I'm going to bed. Hope to hear from you soon!

Alison

B **Think about sports, games, and other activities you enjoy doing.** Then write a response to the email in **A**.

C **Find places to combine sentences in your email.** Then rewrite it.

3

WHAT SHOULD I DO?

PREVIEW

A **Look at the tips for new students.** Circle the correct answers.

TIPS FOR NEW STUDENTS

1 If your laptop isn't working properly, our shop can help you **lend it / get it repaired**.

2 Students without laptops can **talk to their parents / go to the library**. On the second floor, there are special tables with computers they can use.

3 Do you enjoy studying with others? You could **join a study group / hire a tutor**. Many students like the extra support they get from learning with others.

4 If you have a problem with a classmate, you should **apologize / talk to a counselor**. Our staff can help solve a variety of problems.

B **Match the problems with the advice.**

Problem

1 My sister is being bullied at school. ○

2 I'm getting poor grades at school. ○

3 My brother doesn't know what career to pursue. ○

4 I told my mother her jacket looked ugly. ○

Advice

○ **a** Have you thought about getting a tutor to help you?

○ **b** You should apologize.

○ **c** He could try talking to some of his teachers.

○ **d** Why doesn't she talk to the principal?

C **Write.** Write a tip for a new student at your school.

_____

LANGUAGE FOCUS

A **Complete the conversation.** Circle the correct answers.

Luiz: Can I get some advice? I have an extra ticket to a soccer game. I know both my girlfriend and my brother want to go. What ¹ **could** / **should** I do?

Shin: Well, have you tried ² **get** / **getting** another ticket?

Luiz: Yeah, but the game is already sold out.

Shin: Why don't you ³ **tell** / **telling** both of them that there's just one extra ticket? Then you ⁴ **could** / **would** let them decide who goes.

Luiz: Ha! I don't think that will work.

Shin: I know! You ⁵ **should** / **would** give one ticket to your brother and the other to your girlfriend.

Luiz: But wait! Then I can't go.

B **Rewrite each piece of advice a different way.**

1	You should tell him the truth.	Why don't _you tell him the truth_ ?
2	Why don't you apologize?	You could _____ .
3	You could try talking to someone.	You should _____ .
4	You could get a tutor.	Have you _____ ?
5	You shouldn't say anything.	If I _____ .

C **Complete the conversation.** Put the sentences in the correct order (1–8).

a __1__ You look upset, Greg. Is everything OK?

b _____ Yes, but I just made it worse!

c _____ Fourth Street? Thanks. I'll go there now.

d __3__ Oh, no! Have you tried cleaning it?

e _____ That's a good idea. Is there one nearby?

f _____ Yes, I think there's one on Fourth Street.

g _____ Well, you could take it to a dry cleaner.

h _____ Not really. I borrowed my friend's jacket yesterday, and I spilled tomato juice all over it.

THE REAL WORLD

A high school student gets advice from a teacher.

A **Skim the discussion thread.** Add these sentences (**a**–**c**) to the correct places (1–3).

> **a** Everyone needs friends. **b** It's not that easy to do! **c** I should have been true to myself.

Message Board

What's the worst advice you've ever gotten? Submitted 2 weeks ago

---

Posted: 3:55 p.m. by **nkdexter** **Reply**

I hate to say it, but it was from my father. He usually gives great advice, but last year I changed schools, and I didn't know anyone there. He said, "Don't bother making friends. Just study." I didn't take his advice.
1 _____

> **MauriceCarre**
> My father also gave me bad advice once. I love painting, and my dream has always been to be an artist. My father suggested I quit being an artist and get a job as an art teacher. I did, and I made more money, but I wasn't happy.

Posted: 3:59 p.m. by **winniemay16** **Reply**

The worst advice? That's easy. I was having a hard time at a new school, and a teacher told me to try and fit in more. I tried to, but it only made things worse because I wasn't being myself. 2 _____

Posted: 4:05 p.m. by **sammylopez** **Reply**

Sometimes I'm not happy about something, and it shows. My sister usually says something like, "You should smile more. It's a bad day, not a bad life." That's easier said than done, though.

> **celia123**
> I know what you mean. I get really nervous before exams. My teacher always says, "Just relax."
> 3 _____

B **Read the discussion thread.** Match the people with the descriptions.

1 nkdexter ○   ○ **a** gave up on a dream

2 MauriceCarre ○   ○ **b** ignored a parent's advice

3 winniemay16 ○   ○ **c** got advice from a sibling

4 sammylopez ○   ○ **d** was told by a teacher to take it easy

5 celia123 ○   ○ **e** tried to be like other people

READING

A **Skim the article.** Choose the best alternative title.

a How to Consider Advice   **b** How to Ask for Advice   **c** How to Take Advice

THE ART OF ASKING FOR ADVICE

A Asking for advice can be scary. In a recent study, 74 percent of participants said they were afraid to ask for advice. But people who ask for advice are more likely to succeed at a task. So how do you ask for advice? Here are a few tips.

B Look for the best person to give you advice. It might be easy to ask all your social media contacts for advice at once, but will you value all advice equally? Probably not. It might be better to target one or two people whose opinions you value the most. Ideally, you want to ask for advice from people who have experience in the topic you're asking about.

C Provide context. For example, imagine you can't decide how to organize a class presentation. When you ask for advice, you should mention the topic, the audience, and the time allowed. You should also consider when to ask. If what you are asking requires a lot of thought, you should approach the person when they are most clear-headed.

D Be specific in your questioning. Imagine you want to own a business someday. Do you ask a business owner, "What advice do you have for me?" No, because it's not specific enough. Instead, try asking, "What college classes did you find helpful for starting a business?"

E Sometimes, you may need to ask for a second opinion. If you can't solve your problem by following the first person's advice, why not ask someone else who may have a different perspective? The key is: Don't be afraid to ask for advice.

B **Answer the questions about *The Art of Asking for Advice*.**

1 DETAIL What is true about three-quarters of the study's participants?

a They didn't like to receive advice.

b They were scared to ask for advice.

c They were worried about getting bad advice.

2 INFERENCE What might be wrong with the question, "What's your advice?"

    a It's too general.   **b** It's too personal.   **c** It's impossible to answer.

3 VOCABULARY What does the word *perspective* in paragraph E mean?

    a set of facts   **b** aim or goal   **c** point of view

4 DETAIL Which tip is NOT discussed in the article?

    a Ask at the right time.   **b** Return the favor.   **c** Ask the right person.

5 COHESION The following sentence would best be placed at the end of which paragraph?

For example, if you want to lose weight, you could ask a fitness trainer for advice on how to do it.

    a paragraph B   **b** paragraph C   **c** paragraph D

C **EXAM PRACTICE** **Check (✓) the sentences the author would probably agree with.**

  a ☐ Ask as many people as you can for advice.

  b ☐ Choose the right time to ask.

  c ☐ Have a list of specific questions.

  d ☐ Give detailed background information.

  e ☐ Ask for a second opinion.

  f ☐ Ask only questions that can be answered with *Yes* or *No*.

VOCABULARY

A **Match the words with their definitions.**

  1 ability   ◯   ◯ **a** slowly; over a long period of time

  2 challenge ◯   ◯ **b** based on facts or situations as they really are

  3 gradually ◯   ◯ **c** something that needs great effort to be done successfully

  4 organization ◯   ◯ **d** a person whose behavior is copied by others

  5 realistic   ◯   ◯ **e** the skill or power needed to do something

  6 role model ◯   ◯ **f** a group of people who work together for a common purpose

B **Complete the conversations.** Circle the correct answers.

  1 **A:** What do you make **for** / **of** / **up** our new teacher?

      B: She seems really cool.

  2 **A:** Why did he just give her a gift?

      B: He wanted to make up **for** / **out** / **of** forgetting her birthday.

  3 **A:** What's that in the tree?

      B: It could be an animal, but I can't quite make it **for** / **out** / **up**.

WRITING

WRITING TIP **ADDING SUPPORT TO YOUR WRITING**

You can make your writing clearer and easier to understand by adding support such as **examples**, **facts**, **anecdotes**, or **quotes**.

An example:	***For example,*** *if you want to lose weight, you could ask a fitness trainer for advice on how to do it.*
A fact:	*In a recent study,* ***74 percent of participants said they were afraid to ask for advice.***
An anecdote:	*Try to make learning interesting for children.* ***My father used to use board games to teach me vocabulary and math.***
A quote:	*Don't be afraid of doing things differently. As Steve Jobs said,* ***"Innovation distinguishes between a leader and a follower."***

A **Read the email below.** Look at the underlined sentences and write the type of support (example, fact, anecdote, or quote) used in each.

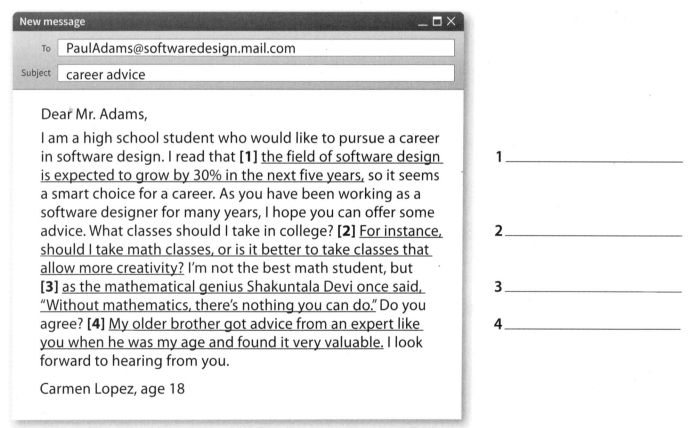

New message

To PaulAdams@softwaredesign.mail.com

Subject career advice

Dear Mr. Adams,

I am a high school student who would like to pursue a career in software design. I read that **[1]** the field of software design is expected to grow by 30% in the next five years, so it seems a smart choice for a career. As you have been working as a software designer for many years, I hope you can offer some advice. What classes should I take in college? **[2]** For instance, should I take math classes, or is it better to take classes that allow more creativity? I'm not the best math student, but **[3]** as the mathematical genius Shakuntala Devi once said, "Without mathematics, there's nothing you can do." Do you agree? **[4]** My older brother got advice from an expert like you when he was my age and found it very valuable. I look forward to hearing from you.

Carmen Lopez, age 18

1 _____

2 _____

3 _____

4 _____

B **Think of a problem you would like advice on.** Create an outline for the email (see **Unit 1**). Include examples, facts, anecdotes, or quotes to add support to your writing.

C **Write your email.**

4

THE KOALA WAS TAKEN TO A SHELTER

PREVIEW

A Match the words with their definitions.

1 attach ○	○ **a**	to put
2 calm down ○	○ **b**	to join or fasten
3 treat ○	○ **c**	to let go, often into the wild
4 place ○	○ **d**	to relax
5 release ○	○ **e**	to give medical care

B Complete the paragraph. Use the words in the box.

> attached   driven   released   treated   washed   wrapped

When a koala gets injured, a vet is usually soon on the scene. When the vet arrives, the koala is

first [1] _____ in a blanket. It's then placed inside a cage and [2] _____ to the shelter.

At the shelter, the koala is [3] _____ so its fur is clean. After that, the animal is checked

and [4] _____ for injuries. The shelter will continue to care for the animal until it's

[5] _____ back into the wild. A tag is often [6] _____ to the koala before it's released.

C Write one fact you know about koalas.

_____

LANGUAGE FOCUS

A Complete the story. Use the correct form of the verbs in parentheses.

It was a cold, dark night. A small squirrel with a broken leg [1] _____ (**find**) outside the animal shelter just before closing time. The creature was dirty and looked cold, so it [2] _____ (**give**) a warm bath by Layla, the shelter vet. Its leg [3] _____ (**treat**), and the squirrel [4] _____ (**wrap**) in a blanket. However, it didn't move, so Layla [5] _____ (**decide**) to give it some water. She [6] _____ (**go**) to get the water, but when she came back, the squirrel wasn't there! Where was it? Layla [7] _____ (**run**) outside and saw the squirrel limping toward a tree. It [8] _____ (**greet**) by another squirrel—maybe its mother!

B Read the sentences. Then rewrite them using the passive form.

1 They're taking the dog to the shelter. *The dog is being taken to the shelter.*

2 Someone saw two bears near the lake. _____

3 Someone released the koala. _____

4 Someone treated the injured owl. _____

5 They're tagging the injured animals. _____

C Complete the conversation. Put the sentences in the correct order (1–7).

a _____ Yeah, one of the teachers took it there.

b _____ That's the plan. They hope its mother is still in the area.

c _____ I did hear that. The poor thing. Did someone take it to the animal shelter?

d _____ I don't think so. I think it was just scared.

e _____ That's good. Was it hurt?

f __1__ Did you hear? A baby fox was found behind the school yesterday!

g __6__ Maybe it got separated from its mother. Are they going to release it?

A baby fox

THE REAL WORLD

National Geographic Photo Ark founder Joel Sartore with a Chinese water dragon

A **Skim the article below.** How was the National Geographic Photo Ark successful?

a It allowed a species to breed in captivity.

b It helped raise awareness of a species' decline.

c It allowed scientists to learn about a new species.

| Home | **BLOG** | Photos | Contact | About Me |

Photo Ark Success Story

By Joel Sartore

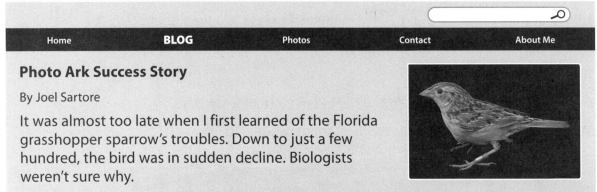

It was almost too late when I first learned of the Florida grasshopper sparrow's troubles. Down to just a few hundred, the bird was in sudden decline. Biologists weren't sure why.

In 2012, writer Ted Williams, biologist Paul Miller, and I traveled to Kissimmee Prairie Preserve State Park in Florida. A singing male grasshopper sparrow was seen defending his mating territory. Paul caught the bird, and I put it in my little photo box. And with that, the Florida grasshopper sparrow was on board the National Geographic Photo Ark.

A year later, *Audubon* magazine put the bird on its cover with the words, "End of the Line?" Between that and social media, people started to take notice of this tiny bird. The U.S. Fish and Wildlife Service has provided over a million dollars to help fight the bird's extinction. Intensive study and perhaps even captive breeding can now begin.

The Photo Ark has done its job.

B Read the article. Match the people and organizations with their actions.

1 Paul Miller ○   ○ **a** gave money to protect the bird

2 Joel Sartore ○   ○ **b** published a photo of the bird

3 *Audubon* magazine ○   ○ **c** photographed the bird

4 U.S. Fish and Wildlife Service ○ ○ **d** caught the bird

READING

A Scan paragraph A. Underline the names of two countries in Africa.

SAVING DUNIA

A She may look like any other gorilla, but Dunia is special. When she was still a baby, some hunters wanted to sell her as a pet. She was caught in Africa, in the Democratic Republic of the Congo. Then, she was put in a sports bag and taken to nearby Rwanda to a man who said that he would buy her. Luckily, this man was actually working with the police, and he drove Dunia to the Mountain Gorilla Veterinary Project, an organization that cares for the area's 700 or so wild mountain gorillas.

B When the people at the project saw Dunia, they knew she wasn't well. She needed food, so she was given green beans, pineapple, bananas, and milk. The project members knew she needed more than food, though. According to project vet Chris Whittier, baby gorillas can't survive if they aren't held by their mothers. The project members gave Dunia around-the-clock care and took turns holding her. It wasn't easy at first. Dunia tried to get away and resisted attention. "Dunia needed contact, but there was no reason that she should trust people after what she'd been through," Whittier says. "Humans had killed her family."

C After six months of loving care, Dunia was finally starting to look like a happy, healthy baby gorilla. However, when she got scared, she would still run back to the people who were caring for her, just like she would to her mother. Over time, Dunia started to go out farther and for longer periods of time. Eventually, the project members were able to return Dunia to the Democratic Republic of the Congo and release her into a gorilla sanctuary.

B Answer the questions about *Saving Dunia*.

1 GIST What could be another title for this article?

   a An Animal Rescue Mission   **b** Gorilla Hunters   **c** Building Gorillas a Home

2 PURPOSE What is the main purpose of paragraph B?

   a to explain why baby gorillas need their parents

   b to describe the care Dunia was given

   c to list what foods baby gorillas like to eat

3 VOCABULARY The word *resisted* in paragraph B can be replaced with _____ .

    a needed   **b** showed she wanted   **c** avoided

4 CAUSE-EFFECT According to Chris Whittier, why was it hard for Dunia to trust people?

    a because human love can't replace a mother's love

    b because too many people took turns holding her

    c because her family had been killed by humans

5 DETAIL Where was Dunia released?

    a into the wild   **b** into a protected area   **c** the article doesn't say

C   **EXAM PRACTICE**   **Complete the summary.** Use words from the article.

Some hunters wanted to make money by selling Dunia, a baby gorilla, as a [1] _____ .
A man in Rwanda agreed to [2] _____ her. He took her to the Mountain Gorilla Veterinary
Project. The people there gave Dunia lots of fruits and vegetables. But she needed more than
food; she needed love. A baby gorilla can't [3] _____ unless it's held by its mother. The
project members took turns [4] _____ Dunia and soon, she began to look happy and
[5] _____ again. She was eventually released into a gorilla sanctuary.

VOCABULARY

A **Complete the sentences.** Use the words in the box.

> cheered   dangerous   frightened   hang   investigate   suddenly

1 It's very _____ for wild animals to cross busy highways.

2 We were driving down the road when, _____ , a deer appeared in front of us.

3 We _____ when the firefighter brought the dog out from the burning building.

4 I'm going to _____ a photo of my family on the living room wall.

5 The police came to _____ a claim that a man is keeping illegal wildlife in his home.

6 The _____ cat refused to come down from the tree.

B **Read the sentences.** Underline each verb. Then check (✓) if it's transitive or intransitive.

	Transitive	Intransitive
1 The firefighter rescued the horses.	☐	☐
2 My package finally arrived.	☐	☐
3 I always help my neighbors.	☐	☐
4 Several people came early.	☐	☐

WRITING

WRITING TIP **USING SENSORY DETAILS**

When you describe an event or tell a story, use sensory details to help paint a picture for the reader. These kinds of details appeal to our five senses.

Sight:	*light blue water, big round eyes, a child smiling sweetly*
Smell:	*salty air, fresh bread, burning meat*
Hearing:	*birds chirping, cried loudly, a howling wind*
Taste:	*sour milk, strong tea, spicy chicken*
Touch:	*cool water, hot sun, a hand on my shoulder*

A Read the beginning and end of the story. Write which of the five senses is used for each underlined phrase.

Otter Rescue!

Macy Hanson stood in the **[1]** hot sun watching a frightened young otter in the river. The otter was alone and **[2]** crying pitifully for its mother. But its mother was not there. She might have been scared away by the **[3]** loud roar of a passing motorboat. Macy knew she could not catch the young otter on her own. She called a rescue service for help.

1 _____

2 _____

3 _____

After the otter was safe in the pool, she was given some **[4]** sweet milk. The rescue team then rushed her to a zoo. The young otter needed several months of care. She was introduced to an older female otter. This female acted as her mother. After three months together, the young otter and her new mother were lifted into a **[5]** black truck and driven to a nearby river, where they were released. The rescue team **[6]** cheered loudly as the two otters swam happily away.

4 _____

5 _____

6 _____

B Think about what happened in the middle of the story. Make some notes.

C Use your notes from B to write the middle of the story. Include sensory details to make your story more interesting.

5

HOW ARE THEY MADE?

PREVIEW

A Complete the paragraph. Use the words in the box.

> flat   grooves   lead   machine   sold   stuck

To make pencils, soft wood is first cut into [1] _____ pieces. Long [2] _____ are then cut into the wood, and the [3] _____ is put in. Another piece of wood is placed on top. The two pieces of wood are [4] _____ together using glue. These are then cut into individual pencils by a [5] _____ . Next, an eraser is added to each pencil. It's now complete! Before the pencils are packaged and [6] _____ , each one is checked carefully by hand.

B Write the past participle of these verbs.

1 see   _____seen_____

2 place   _____

3 check   _____

4 cut   _____

5 add   _____

6 make   _____

7 sell   _____

8 put   _____

9 design   _____

10 choose _____

C Write. Besides pencils, what other types of stationery do you use in class? Name three things.

_____

LANGUAGE FOCUS

A Complete the information. Circle the correct answers.

Kids [1] **love / are loved** lollipops, but have you ever thought about how lollipops [2] **make / are made**? It's a simple process. First, sugar, water, and corn syrup [3] **mix / are mixed** together by a machine. This mixture [4] **heated / is heated** until the temperature [5] **reaches / is reached** 150°C. Next, coloring and flavors [6] **add / are added**, and the mixture [7] **pours / is poured** into molds. Then a factory worker [8] **places / is placed** a stick in each mold. Finally, the lollipops [9] **remove / are removed** from their molds and [10] **wrap / wrapped** in plastic.

B Read the sentences. Then rewrite them using the passive form + *by*.

1 Chemists test the flavors and colors. _____

2 Factory workers wrap the lollipops. _____

3 A supervisor checks each lollipop. _____

4 Kids of all ages love the sweet treats. _____

C Complete the conversation with the correct form of the verbs in parentheses.
Use contractions where possible.

Ling: I really like your scarf. Is it new?

Sarah: Yeah, I [1] _____ (**get**) it last month when I was in Thailand. It [2] _____ (**make**) of silk.

Ling: It's very pretty. And it [3] _____ (**feel**) so soft.

Sarah: It [4] _____ (**make**) by hand in northern Thailand. The people there [5] _____ (**produce**) a lot of nice handicrafts. I [6] _____ (**buy**) this scarf directly from the woman who made it.

ARTIFICIAL FLAVORS

A **Skim the article.** Number these questions in the order they are answered (1–3).

a _____ How easy is it to trick the brain?

b _____ How are artificial flavors made?

c _____ What are esters?

If you drank a glass of orange juice a century ago, the juice would have been natural—made from real oranges. These days, however, you may find that the juice is completely artificial or manufactured. Many drink companies today create chemical mixtures that mimic natural flavors.

Some natural flavors are very complex. There may be hundreds of different chemicals interacting to create the smell. Yet many flavors, especially of fruit, have just one or a few main chemicals—called esters—that are responsible for the smell. Different esters have different smells. For example, one ester is the main component for orange flavor. Another is the chief component for banana flavor. If these esters are added to a product, it will smell like an orange or a banana.

The majority of artificial flavors have both smell and taste components. To get the flavor closer to the real thing, other chemicals are often added to esters. This can be done through careful analysis of the real flavor, or in some cases by trial and error.

It's actually very easy to trick the brain. An artificially processed fruit juice can taste as if it has been freshly squeezed if it's created with just the right chemicals. To the brain, a flavor is just chemicals. It doesn't matter if it comes from a real fruit or if it's made in a lab.

B **Read the article.** Circle the correct answers.

1 The word *mimic* in the first paragraph means **copy** / **mix** / **add to**.

2 An ester is a type of **taste cell** / **fruit** / **chemical**.

3 Making artificial flavors is **nearly impossible** / **sometimes done through guessing** / **fairly easy**.

READING

A **Scan the article.** Underline five materials that have been used in 3D printing.

HOW DOES A 3D PRINTER WORK?

A 3D-printing technology is changing the way we produce objects, from coffee cups to toys to musical instruments. It's part of a process known as "additive manufacturing." The process allows designers and manufacturers to produce 3D objects quickly, cheaply, and easily. 3D printers have even been used to create complex structures like bridges and houses. But how exactly does a 3D printer work?

B First, a design of the object is created. You can either create your own designs using modeling software or visit websites that show existing designs. The design is then digitally "cut." During this process, the object is broken down into many layers. After that, the final design is sent to the printer.

C A 3D printer works by pushing melted material through a tiny tube onto a flat surface to dry. The most common material used is plastic. The printer adds layers on top to build up the object—moving both back and forth and up and down—until it is complete. The completed object is then removed from the printer. It may need to be brushed, washed, or polished before it's considered final.

A close-up view of a 3D printer at work

D Many different materials can be used for 3D printing, such as plastic, metal, concrete, or glass—and the list grows longer every day. In the medical world, doctors are using bio-materials to make human body parts, and in the world of food production, 3D printing of food is a growing trend. In 2016, for example, a 3D-printing pop-up restaurant opened in London. Diners were able to order 3D-printed food from a 3D-printed menu, and use 3D-printed plates and glasses on 3D-printed furniture.

B **Answer the questions about *How Does a 3D Printer Work?***

1 INFERENCE Which statement would the author most likely agree with?

  a The medical industry is the largest adopter of 3D-printing technology.

  b 3D printing will play an important part in the future of manufacturing.

  c Most homes will have 3D printers in the next few years.

2 COHESION Where is the best place for this sentence in paragraph A?

This refers to creating an object by adding material layer by layer.

    a after sentence 2   **b** after sentence 3   **c** after sentence 4

3 VOCABULARY What is the meaning of the word *digitally* in paragraph B?

    a in a way that relates to someone's appearance

    b in a way that uses mathematical calculations

    c in a way that uses computer technology

4 DETAIL Which of the following is NOT mentioned as a product that has been 3D printed?

    a bridges   **b** clothing   **c** body parts

5 PURPOSE Why does the writer mention the London pop-up restaurant in paragraph D?

    a to show that 3D printing of food is becoming more achievable

    b to show that 3D printing is considered to be art by some people

    c to show that people can't tell the difference between real and 3D-printed objects

C   **EXAM PRACTICE** **How does a 3D printer work?** Put the steps in order (1–7).

    a _____ The next layers of the object are printed on top.

    b _____ The bottom layer is left to dry.

    c _____ The design is sent to a 3D printer.

    d _____ The object is removed from the printer.

    e __1__ A design is created.

    f _____ Melted material is pushed through a tube to form the bottom layer of the object.

    g _____ The object is brushed, washed, or polished.

VOCABULARY

A **Complete the sentences.** Use the words in the box.

> combine   complex   global   individual   supply   variety

   1 With the increase in overseas sales, the company has built up a(n) _____ presence.

   2 Several countries _____ Nestlé with the cocoa it uses to make chocolate.

   3 The process of manufacturing car tires is surprisingly _____ .

   4 Each _____ step in the production of chewing gum requires time and patience.

   5 To make hard candy at home, you usually need to _____ sugar and corn syrup.

   6 This ice cream comes in a(n) _____ of tropical flavors.

B **Complete the sentences.** Circle the correct answers.

1 The company's global **awareness** / **network** allows it to sell its products all over the world.

2 Everyone has heard of the company Samsung. It's a well-known global **warming** / **brand**.

3 Let's post a video to raise global **brand** / **awareness** of the dangers of single-use plastics.

4 Many people feel that global **warming** / **network** is the biggest threat to the planet today.

WRITING

WRITING TIP INFORMAL AND FORMAL WRITING

When you write, think about what type of text you are writing and who is going to read it. This will tell you how formal your writing should be.

INFORMAL WRITING	FORMAL WRITING
Personal emails, text messages, blogs	News articles, essays, business letters
Use of abbreviations and contractions	No abbreviations or contractions
Short and simple sentences	Long and more complex sentences
Use of slang, phrasal verbs, and idioms	No slang, phrasal verbs, or idioms
Less use of passive voice	More use of passive voice

A **Below is an article from a student newsletter.** Underline all the examples of the passive voice. What other examples of formal writing do you see? Tell a partner.

There are many delicious street foods that I enjoy, but my favorite is *taiyaki*. It is a Japanese snack that is shaped like a fish. It is made by pouring a batter into both sides of a mold. A filling such as sweet red bean paste is added to one side of the mold and is pressed halfway into the batter. Then the mold is closed, and the snack is cooked on a low heat until it is golden brown in color. *Taiyaki* is often available at festivals, and it tastes especially good on a cold winter day.

B **Imagine you are writing an article about your favorite street food for your school newspaper.** What kind of food is it? How is it made? List the steps and other interesting information about the food.

C **Use your notes from B to write an article about the street food.** Use a formal tone.

6

LOOK AT THOSE NARWHALS!

PREVIEW

A Match. Read the descriptions (1–4). Then write the names of the animals from the box.

> dugong   king crab   narwhal   seahorse

1 I live in the Arctic Ocean. I have a tusk, which is very long. I'm known as the "unicorn of the sea." What am I? _____

2 I'm a tiny type of fish that uses my tail to grasp objects. I'm named after another, larger animal that I look like. I like warm climates. What am I? _____

3 I can be found in the Pacific and Arctic Oceans. I have a blue, red, or brown shell. Unfortunately for me, I'm a popular food. What am I? _____

4 I'm a gentle mammal that's also known as a "sea cow." I use my flippers to steer in the water. I live in the warm waters of the Indian and Pacific Oceans. What am I? _____

B Choose one of the animals below. Write a description of it, similar to those in **A**.

> crocodile   dolphin   penguin   turtle

_____

_____

LANGUAGE FOCUS

A **Complete the sentences.** Circle the correct answers.

1 Clownfish, **which** / **who** are usually orange and white, live in small groups.

2 My parents, **which** / **who** are scuba diving instructors, support marine conservation.

3 Sally, **which** / **who** is a volunteer at the zoo, is very interested in animals.

4 The Great Barrier Reef, **which** / **who** is home to many marine species, is popular with divers.

B **Rewrite these sentences about Antarctica.** Use *which* or *who*.

1 Antarctica is the coldest continent on Earth. It's always covered in ice and snow.

Antarctica, which is always covered in ice and snow, is the coldest

continent on Earth.

2 The emperor penguin lives only in Antarctica. It's the largest penguin in the world.

_____

_____

3 Captain James Cook died in 1779. He was the first explorer to sail around Antarctica.

_____

_____

C **Complete the conversation.** Put the sentences in the correct order (1–6).

a _____ I think my friend Matt spent some time in that area. He really enjoyed it.

b _____ What a fun job! I wish I had a job like that.

c _1_ My cousin Carrie, who's about your age, is coming to visit. You should meet her while she's here.

d _____ I'd love to! Are you two very close?

e _____ I'm sure he did. It's a popular place for tourists. Anyway, Carrie works for an adventure travel company. She takes people out on boats in the bay.

f _____ Yeah, she's my favorite cousin. She's from New Zealand. She lives in the Bay of Islands, which is a very pretty part of the country.

Bay of Islands, New Zealand

A swimmer tests a new swimsuit designed to increase speed.

A   Skim the article. Choose the best title.

a The Beauty of Sharks   **b** Design by Nature   **c** Why Sharks Have Scales

Sharks may be known for their teeth, but it's their scales that are getting more attention these days. Shark scales have provided an inspiration for design.

When viewed under a microscope, the skin of a shark is made up of countless tiny scales. These scales, which point toward the tail, allow the shark to swim through water smoothly and quickly with less drag.

A swimsuit manufacturer created material that uses a similar design. A swimsuit made of this fabric received a lot of attention at the 2004 Olympics, when American swimmer Michael Phelps wore a sharkskin-inspired swimsuit that covered most of his body. Many people said the suit gave him the winning edge. At the next Olympics, in 2008, 98 percent of medal winners wore sharkskin-inspired swimsuits that reached from the shoulders to the calves.

The new suits had a dramatic impact on the sport of swimming, as record after record began to fall. In 2010, the International Swimming Federation voted to ban the use of these full-body suits during competition. Today, male swimmers are only allowed to wear sharkskin-inspired suits from the waist to the knee, and female swimmers from the shoulder to the knee.

B   Read the article. Circle **T** for true or **F** for false.

1	A shark's scales help it to swim fast.	**T**	**F**
2	Designers created swimsuits from real shark scales.	**T**	**F**
3	Some people think that a sharkskin-inspired swimsuit gives its wearer an unfair advantage.	**T**	**F**
4	Today, swimmers can compete in full-body sharkskin-inspired suits.	**T**	**F**

READING

A **Skim the article.** What is the main idea of the article?

   a Artificial reefs are attracting tourists.

   b Subway cars are polluting the ocean.

   c Subway cars are being used to create artificial reefs.

SUBWAY SHELTER

A Along the Atlantic coast of the United States, thousands of fish are crowded into subway cars. But these cars are going nowhere, and fishermen couldn't be happier. The subway cars were placed in the ocean to serve as artificial reefs.

B In 2001, New York City transportation officials wanted to recycle more than a thousand subway cars. The artificial reef program seemed like an ideal solution. Before the rail cars were sunk, all dangerous materials were removed. The doors and windows were taken off, and the interiors were cleaned. What remained were 9,000-kilogram boxes with good water circulation and lots of areas for fish to hide in. The cars were then dropped from ships, and they sank to the ocean floor. More than 1,200 cars were dropped into the ocean.

C Hard surfaces—whether natural or human-made—are attractive to clams, mussels, and other food sources important to local fish populations. But most of the ocean floor along the mid-Atlantic is bare sand. "In the mid-Atlantic region, we have very, very little exposed rock," said Jeff Tinsman, who coordinated the placement of the subway cars. These artificial reefs therefore quickly attracted marine life. Divers to the reefs often report seeing hundreds of black sea bass, which feed on mussels, clams, and small fish.

D Each year, fish and wildlife agencies in the region release guides for the artificial reefs. Fishermen use these to find the best fishing spots. Local agencies manage reef fish populations the same way they do any other fishery, setting limits on the size and number of fish that can be caught.

E More than 2,500 subway cars were dropped into the Atlantic Ocean before the project officially ended in 2010. However, the effects are still evident today. The subway car reefs have helped to create thriving new habitats for varied sea life where once the seabed was just sand. Michael Zacchea, who oversaw the recycling of the subway cars, said the project has been "more successful than we ever considered it would be."

B **Answer the questions about *Subway Shelter*.**

   1 DETAIL Why do recycled subway cars make good artificial reefs?

     a They have hard surfaces.   **b** They have glass windows.   **c** There are few places to hide.

   2 INFERENCE Which marine creatures were probably attracted to the cars first?

     a black sea bass   **b** mussels and clams   **c** sharks

3 PURPOSE What is the main purpose of paragraph C?

    a to describe why clams and mussels are found all over the Atlantic

    b to compare the different marine creatures that can be found in the Atlantic Ocean

    c to explain why the mid-Atlantic was a good choice for the reef program

4 DETAIL How many subway cars were dropped into the ocean over the course of the project?

    a 1,000   **b** just over 1,200   **c** more than 2,500

5 DETAIL What is NOT true about the artificial reef program?

    a Fishermen are allowed to fish near the reef.

    b The program is still in operation today.

    c Local agencies manage the fish population on the reef.

C   **EXAM PRACTICE**   **Complete the summary.** Use words from the article.

On the Atlantic coast of the United States, thousands of [1] _____ cars from New York

City were dropped into the ocean to create artificial reefs. All the doors, windows, and other

[2] _____ materials were first removed from each car. The interiors were then

[3] _____ thoroughly. In the mid-Atlantic region, there is little exposed [4] _____,

so the cars act as a hard surface to attract marine life. Local agencies manage the reef fish

population by setting limits on the size and [5] _____ _____ of fish that fishermen can catch.

On the whole, the artificial reef program has been very [6] _____.

VOCABULARY

A **Complete the sentences.** Use the words in the box.

> attract   damage   popular   remains   shallow   warn

  1 Several types of fish _____ their prey by using light.

  2 The Great Barrier Reef is a(n) _____ tourist spot.

  3 Both water pollution and global warming _____ coral reefs.

  4 The lifeguard tried to _____ the swimmers that a shark was nearby.

  5 The outer wall is all that _____ of the ancient temple.

  6 I'm comfortable swimming in _____ water, but deep water makes me nervous.

B **Rewrite these sentences using the words in parentheses.**

  1 He saw 10 sharks in the water. (***more than***) _____

  2 I've gone diving a dozen times. (***nearly***) _____

3 We caught 20 fish on our trip. (*or so*) _____

4 There are 60 fish in the tank. (*about*) _____

WRITING

WRITING TIP **ADDING VARIETY WITH SYNONYMS**

To make your writing more interesting, use synonyms so you don't repeat the same word many times. Note the synonyms in the sentences below.

> The **injured** animal was able to **quickly** escape the hunter. Although it was **hurt**, it was still able to run **fast**.
>
> The **little fish** needed to find a **place** to hide before the shark **found** it. After it **discovered** the perfect **spot**, the **tiny creature** did not move until the shark swam away.

A Read the notice below. Find a synonym in the paragraph for each **bold** word.

talk _____   big _____   struck _____

spilled _____   occurred _____   protect _____

> ## You Can Help
>
> Marine animals can't **talk**, but if they could speak to us, they would probably ask us to help protect them from oil spills. Oil spills happen when **big** ships that carry oil—called tankers—become damaged and leak oil into the ocean. On March 24, 1989, one of these huge tankers, called the *Exxon Valdez*, **struck** Bligh Reef in Alaska. After it hit the reef, oil **spilled** into the ocean. On April 20, 2010, another oil spill **occurred**, this time in the Gulf of Mexico. This spill was caused by an explosion on an offshore oil rig and its subsequent sinking. Oil leaked into the water for nearly three months. These are just two of the biggest oil spills that have ever happened! You can help **protect** animals from oil spills through various ways. For example, you could support leaders who want to preserve our natural resources, and who are against drilling for oil in our oceans.

B Research a cause that is important to you. Choose one of the following or your own idea. Take notes on what your cause is and what people can do to help.

- stopping overfishing

- reducing pollution in rivers

- protecting endangered animal species

C Use your notes from B to write a paragraph about your cause. Then review the paragraph and look for places to add variety by using synonyms.

7

Ruins of an ancient temple in Sudan

IT MIGHT
HAVE BEEN A TEMPLE

PREVIEW

A Complete the sentences. Use the words in the box.

> bones   buried   fight   gold   legend

1 The archeologists found human _____ with marks on them all over the site, suggesting

   that a deadly _____ had taken place there.

2 An ancient _____ says that the city was abandoned by its people because of a

   10-year drought.

3 The treasure that the explorers found was _____ two meters under a tree. It contained

   mostly silver and _____ coins.

B Cross out the odd item in each group.

1 tribe	gold	treasure	coins
2 scientist	archeologist	ruins	researcher
3 legend	machine	story	mystery
4 temple	religion	invader	god

C Write. Choose one of the odd items from **B**. Write a sentence using that word.

_____

LANGUAGE FOCUS

A **Complete the sentences.** Use the correct form of the words in parentheses.

1 The ancient king _____ (**might / die**) from a war injury.

2 This weapon _____ (**can't / be**) made of gold. Gold is much heavier than this.

3 The river _____ (**could / dry up**) because of a drought in the 1880s.

4 The treasure _____ (**might not / be**) here anymore. Robbers

   _____ (**might / steal**) it.

B **Match the observations with the guesses.**

Observations	Guesses
1 There's a laptop on the desk. ○	○ **a** It might be for a party.
2 The ground here is very wet. ○	○ **b** It must have been printed a long time ago.
3 The photo has turned yellow. ○	○ **c** It must have rained earlier.
4 There's a big meal on the table. ○	○ **d** It could be Lisa's. She was studying here just now.

C **Complete the conversation.** Circle the correct answers.

Todd: Look at this ancient coin I got on my trip to Italy!

Tanya: Wow! Do you know who the man on the coin is?

Todd: It [1] **can't / must** be Julius Caesar. The image looks just like him. And his name is here in Latin. You know, Cleopatra lived at the same time as Caesar. She [2] **could / must** have held this same coin!

Tanya: Yes, that's possible. Is the coin made of gold?

Todd: Well, it [3] **could / can't** be gold. Or it [4] **might / must** be bronze. I'm not sure.

Tanya: So where did you find it?

Todd: Oh, I didn't find it. I bought it from a guy on the street—for three euros.

Tanya: Oh, no! I think he [5] **should / might** have cheated you. A real Roman coin would be worth much more than that!

A collection of ancient Roman coins

THE REAL WORLD

LOST TO HISTORY

A statue of Genghis Khan in Mongolia

A Scan the article. Write the dates for these events.

1 Fortress found: _____

2 Fortress most likely built: _____

A team of archeologists has confirmed that an old fortress in southwest Mongolia was built by the Mongol leader Genghis Khan. The fortress, which was discovered in 2001, measures 170 meters by 200 meters, and has thick walls made of hard soil. Archeologists uncovered animal bones, wood fragments, and Chinese ceramics at the site.

In 2014, archeologists used carbon dating to date these artifacts to between the 12th and 14th centuries. They concluded that the fortress must have been a military base during Genghis Khan's invasion of Central Asia. They believe that the base was probably built in 1212 and was used as Khan expanded his army westward. After the decline of the Mongol Empire in the 14th century, the fortress fell into ruin. It eventually became lost to history.

Koichi Matsuda, professor of Mongol Empire history at Osaka International University, was the expedition's team leader. He hopes the discovery will provide new information about the history of this region of Mongolia between the 13th and 14th centuries.

B Read the article. Choose the correct answers.

1 Another title for this article could be _____ .

    a The Death of Genghis Khan   **b** The Mongol Empire   **c** An Ancient Fortress

2 Which of the following was NOT discovered at the site?

    a bones   **b** gold coins   **c** pieces of wood

3 The military base probably fell into ruin because the Mongols _____ it.

    a destroyed   **b** stopped using   **c** buried

READING

A Skim the article. Check (✓) all the questions that the article answers.

a ☐ When did the Moche control northern Peru?

b ☐ What was found in the tomb with the mummy?

c ☐ How long did it take to build the tomb?

d ☐ Was the mummy a man or a woman?

e ☐ What do the mummy's tattoos mean?

THE MYSTERY OF THE MUMMY

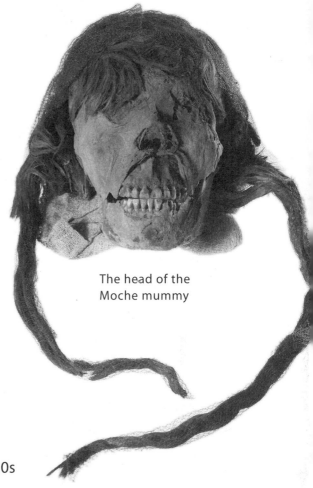

The head of the Moche mummy

A Inside an ancient building in Peru, archeologists found a tomb. The tomb was built by the Moche, a civilization that controlled northern Peru from A.D. 100 to 800.

B After digging carefully for several weeks, the team of archeologists found one of the world's best-preserved mummies. It was buried with gold nose rings, necklaces, and weapons that were usually used by the best soldiers. Based on this, the team assumed that the mummy must have been a powerful man. However, when the gold bowl that was covering the mummy's face was removed, they were surprised to see that the mummy wasn't a man at all. It was actually a young woman, who was probably in her 20s when she died.

Multiple Questions

C The archeologists were excited, but now they had even more questions. This was an unusual mummy—the first discovery of its kind. Sixteen centuries ago in Peru, women were not considered very important in society. So who was this mummy? She was put in the tomb with all these treasures, so she couldn't have been a regular person. Was she a queen? Was she married to someone important? She was also unusual because she had tattoos—drawings on the skin of her arms, legs, and feet. The tattoos showed images of animals like snakes, spiders, and crabs. Were the tattoos religious in nature? The experts couldn't understand what these tattoos meant or why the mummy was buried this way.

No Answers

D The archeologists have studied the mummy and the area where they found her, but they still haven't been able to answer most of their questions. For example, the mummy didn't seem to be hurt or sick, so why did she die when she was so young? They don't know yet, but they do know that whoever she was, she must have been very important in her time.

B Answer the questions about *The Mystery of the Mummy*.

1 `DETAIL` What is true about the mummy?

   a It was buried next to a man.

   b It was very well preserved.

   c It was found by local farmers.

2 `REFERENCE` In paragraph B, *they* refers to _____ .

   a the Moche   b soldiers   c archeologists

3 `DETAIL` Why did the archeologists first think the mummy was a powerful man?

   a because of the items that were buried with it

   b because of the position they found the body in

   c because of the tattoos on the body

4 `VOCABULARY` The word *regular* in paragraph C can be replaced with _____ .

   a religious   b special   c ordinary

5 `INFERENCE` What would the archeologists probably be most excited to discover now?

   a more gold jewelry in the tomb

   b marks made by weapons on the woman's bones

   c ancient pottery products near the tomb

C EXAM PRACTICE Read the sentences below. Circle Fa for fact or Th for theory.

1	The mummy was a soldier.	**Fa**	**Th**
2	The mummy was in her 20s when she died.	**Fa**	**Th**
3	The mummy's tattoos showed pictures of animals.	**Fa**	**Th**
4	The mummy was married to an important person.	**Fa**	**Th**
5	The cause of the woman's death remains unknown.	**Fa**	**Th**

VOCABULARY

A Complete the sentences. Use the words in the box.

> abandon   collapse   imagine   lack of   peak   population

1 No one knows why the ancient people chose to _____ the village.

2 A(n) _____ resources hasn't stopped many countries from having strong economies.

3 It's interesting to _____ what the ancient city might have looked like in the past.

4 Archeologists believe that a severe drought led to the civilization's _____ .

5 The _____ in this area has increased greatly since the discovery of gold.

6 The Inca civilization was at the _____ of its power in the 15th century.

B **Complete the sentences.** Circle the correct answers.

1 When they heard the **tsunami / avalanche** warning, they left the beach and went to higher ground.

2 After the **blizzard / flood**, it took weeks for the water level to go down.

3 The strong winds from the **flood / hurricane** caused a lot of damage.

4 The rescue workers were able to save the skiers who were buried by the **hurricane / avalanche**.

WRITING

WRITING TIP **DEVELOPING PARAGRAPHS BY GIVING REASONS**

When stating a theory in a piece of writing, it's important to give reasons to support it. Note the underlined reason the writer gives to support each theory below.

> *The mummy must have been an important person **since** <u>her tomb contained a lot of treasure</u>.*
>
> *These ruins are very important **because** <u>they show that religion is older than civilization</u>.*
>
> *The area was likely the site of a large battle, **as** <u>archeologists found bones and weapons scattered about</u>.*
>
> *<u>The Mayan tomb contained multiple weapons</u>, **so** it might have been the tomb of a soldier.*

A **Read the article about the mummy on page 43 again.** Write a few ideas (theories) about who you think she might have been.

1 The woman could have been a fierce warrior. _____

2 _____

3 _____

B **Choose one of your theories in A.** List two reasons that support your theory. Do additional research if necessary.

1 _____

2 _____

C **Write a short paragraph explaining your theory.** Use your notes from **B**.

Petronas Twin Towers, Malaysia

8

IT'S TALLER THAN THE EIFFEL TOWER!

PREVIEW

A Complete the crossword puzzle. Use the pictures to help you.

Across

2

5

6

7

Down

1

3

4

6

B Look at the photo and title above. What else do you know about the Petronas Twin Towers? Write two facts about it.

1 _____

2 _____

LANGUAGE FOCUS

A Complete the sentences. Circle the correct answers.

1 I love to travel. My **most / more** memorable trip was to Brazil.

2 We didn't go into the Museum of Modern Art. The tickets were **too / enough** expensive.

3 The clock tower is **tall / taller** than the school. It's also **newer / newest**.

4 I think the new museum is just **good enough / as good as** the old one.

B Complete the blog post. Use the correct form of the words in parentheses. Add *the*, *as*, *too*, or *enough* if necessary.

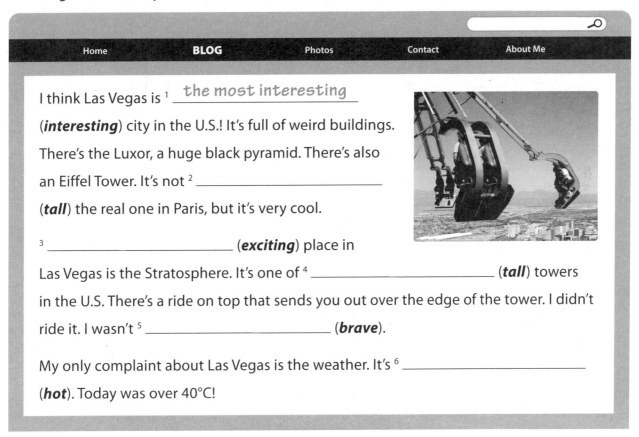

| Home | **BLOG** | Photos | Contact | About Me |

I think Las Vegas is ¹ ___the most interesting___
(*interesting*) city in the U.S.! It's full of weird buildings.
There's the Luxor, a huge black pyramid. There's also
an Eiffel Tower. It's not ² _____
(*tall*) the real one in Paris, but it's very cool.

³ _____ (*exciting*) place in
Las Vegas is the Stratosphere. It's one of ⁴ _____ (*tall*) towers
in the U.S. There's a ride on top that sends you out over the edge of the tower. I didn't
ride it. I wasn't ⁵ _____ (*brave*).

My only complaint about Las Vegas is the weather. It's ⁶ _____
(*hot*). Today was over 40°C!

C Read the conversation and correct four errors.

Rosa: How was Mexico City, Jack?

Jack: It was the goodest vacation I've ever had! I stayed near the Zócalo. I think it's the larger public square in the world.

Rosa: How was the food? Did you try any street food?

Jack: I ate street food all the time. It's not as expensive than the food in the restaurants, and I think it's tastiest.

Rosa: Did you go outside the city?

Jack: I did. I climbed up the Pyramid of the Sun. It's too bad you couldn't come with me.

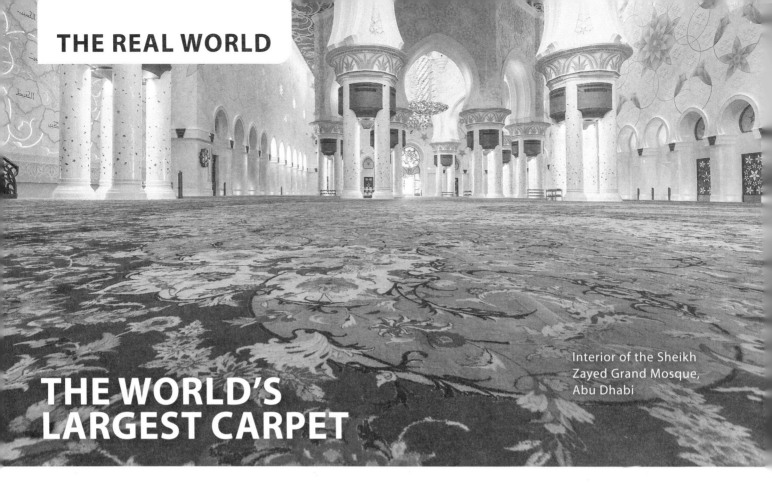

THE REAL WORLD

THE WORLD'S LARGEST CARPET

Interior of the Sheikh Zayed Grand Mosque, Abu Dhabi

A Skim the article. Where was the world's largest carpet woven? _____

When most people enter Abu Dhabi's Sheikh Zayed Grand Mosque, they look up to admire the beautiful domes and minarets. But there is something just as incredible below as well: the world's largest hand-woven carpet.

The Sheikh Zayed Grand Mosque took 11 years to build. Natural materials like marble, ceramics, crystal, and gold were used for much of its construction. Iran, which has a long history of carpet weaving, offered Abu Dhabi's leader a hand-woven carpet for the mosque's main prayer room. Because the mosque is so large, this would be a carpet unlike any other.

The carpet took more than 1,200 weavers about a year and a half to complete. It consists of about 72 percent wool and 28 percent cotton. The finished carpet has 2.2 billion hand-tied knots, and it weighs 12 tons. In total, it's 133 meters long and 43 meters wide. That's bigger than four Olympic-size swimming pools! Because a carpet this size would be too large to move, nine separate carpet pieces had to be created. These pieces were flown to Abu Dhabi to be stitched together, creating the final carpet.

The carpet isn't just huge. It's also full of detail and color. There are flower patterns and a total of 25 different natural colors, including bright reds, greens, and pale creams. The carpet is indeed a wonderful example of design and creativity.

B Read the article. Circle **T** for true, **F** for false, or **NG** for not given.

1	It took longer to create the carpet than to build the mosque.	T	F	NG
2	The carpet is predominantly made from wool.	T	F	NG
3	The carpet is the same size as four Olympic-size swimming pools.	T	F	NG
4	The main color of the final carpet is green.	T	F	NG

READING

A Skim the article. The diagram on the right shows the SMART tunnel during _____ .

a regular use **b** a moderate storm **c** a serious storm

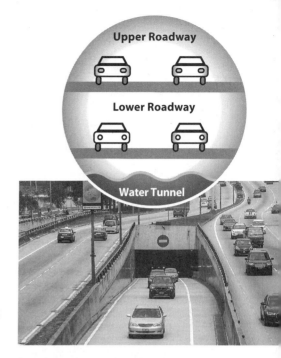

BUILDING SMART

Kuala Lumpur has one of the world's most innovative tunnels—a combined motorway and stormwater tunnel. It's the longest multi-purpose tunnel in the world.

Malaysia's busy capital city of Kuala Lumpur frequently
5 experiences heavy rains. In the past, these rains caused serious flooding in the city center, with the rainwater remaining for up to six hours. The floodwaters damaged property and slowed traffic in the city, resulting in the loss of billions of dollars. To help improve the situation, the government approved the construction of an innovative tunnel—the SMART tunnel.

10 SMART stands for Stormwater Management and Road Tunnel. Construction of the tunnel began in 2003 and was completed in 2007. More than 30,000 motorists use it every day. The tunnel, which cost about half a billion dollars to build, consists of three sections. The upper two sections are roadways. Each allows traffic to move in one direction. The third, lowest section is a stormwater tunnel. When there is little or no rainfall, the roadway
15 sections are open to motorists and the water tunnel is closed.

The SMART system is activated during a moderate storm. The floodwater is directed into the lowest section of the tunnel. The upper sections remain open to traffic. However, during a serious storm, both of the two roadway sections become closed to traffic. After all of the vehicles have left the tunnel, gates are opened to allow the floodwaters into the
20 upper sections. All three channels can then carry the floodwaters away from the city center. Within four days, the entire tunnel is opened to traffic again.

Since its opening, the SMART tunnel has prevented many serious floods from affecting Kuala Lumpur. In fact, a huge storm hit the city only three weeks after the SMART tunnel was completed.

B Answer the questions about _Building SMART_.

1 PURPOSE What is the purpose of the article?

   a to describe how Kuala Lumpur solved its traffic problem

   b to describe a multi-use tunnel that has solved a problem

   c to describe how Malaysia moves floodwaters to rural areas

2 VOCABULARY The word _innovative_ in line 1 means _____ .

   a big and attractive   **b** bright and colorful   **c** original and creative

3 DETAIL The tunnel cost _____ to build.

   a $5 million   **b** $50 million   **c** $500 million

4 DETAIL Where in the tunnel can motorists drive during a severe storm?

    a only in the top section

    b only in the upper two sections

    c They cannot drive anywhere in the tunnel.

5 PURPOSE What is the purpose of the final sentence?

    a to show that storms in Malaysia are unpredictable

    b to show that the tunnel was an immediate success

    c to show that the tunnel was finished earlier than planned

C   EXAM PRACTICE   **Read the statements.** Circle **T** for true, **F** for false, or **NG** for not given.

1 Flooding used to slow down traffic in Kuala Lumpur.	**T**	**F**	**NG**
2 It took over 10 years to build the SMART tunnel.	**T**	**F**	**NG**
3 During a serious storm, the upper sections of the tunnel allow traffic in both directions.	**T**	**F**	**NG**
4 There are plans to build SMART tunnels in other cities in Malaysia.	**T**	**F**	**NG**

VOCABULARY

A **Complete the sentences.** Use the words in the box.

> board   export   goods   region   rely on   transport

1 People often sell their handmade _____ in the local market.

2 Many people now _____ the internet for their daily news.

3 Oil remains the biggest _____ for many Gulf countries.

4 It's always a good idea to _____ your train a few minutes early.

5 This _____ of the country is known for its beautiful lakes.

6 These trains _____ machine parts from the factory to the warehouse.

B **Complete the conversation.** Circle the correct answers.

Iris: Are you ready for your [1] **locals** / **trip** to Italy?

Keiko: I think so. I got my [2] **plane** / **train** ticket the other day. I bought a [3] **one-way** / **round-trip** ticket. I fly out on June 10 and return the night of the 23rd.

Iris: So you'll be there almost two weeks. Nice! Are you flying [4] **passengers** / **first-class**?

Keiko: I wish! I could never afford that. But look here—I just got a new [5] **passport** / **luggage**. Italy will be my first stamp.

Iris: So what are you planning to do in Italy?

Keiko: I'll start in Rome and spend a few days there. Then I'm going to take a [6] **car / tour** of Naples. After that I'll take the [7] **train / local** to Florence. I might rent a [8] **journey / car** there and drive around the area.

Iris: Sounds fun! I'm sure you'll have a great time there.

WRITING

WRITING TIP **ORGANIZING IDEAS IN A CHART**

Putting information in a chart can help you see how ideas relate to each other and help you decide how to organize information. You can put the information into columns and rows, create a word web, or organize the information in an outline.

A **Look at these notes about a famous skyscraper.** Add the information to the chart.

London, England	180 meters tall	nicknamed the Gherkin
in financial district	modern design	cost: £230 million ($300 million)
completed in 2003	looks like a cucumber	also known as 30 St. Mary Axe

Building name	
Location	
Appearance/Height	
Year completed	
Cost to build	

B **Choose another skyscraper you know about.** Research key information about it and complete the chart below.

Building name	
Location	
Appearance/Height	
Year completed	
Cost to build	

C **Use the information in the two charts above to write a paragraph.** Compare the two skyscrapers.

Actor Leonardo DiCaprio

9

HE'S A GREAT ACTOR, ISN'T HE?

PREVIEW

A   Complete the chart with the words from the box.

dull	exciting	gorgeous	interesting
overrated	predictable	superb	unrealistic

Positive words	Negative words

B   Match the words with their definitions.

1 plot   ○   ○ **a** clothes worn by actors

2 special effects ○   ○ **b** the person an actor plays

3 costumes   ○   ○ **c** what happens in a book, TV show, or film

4 soundtrack   ○   ○ **d** the music for a film or TV show

5 character   ○   ○ **e** unusual pictures or sounds that are created for film and other media by using particular equipment

C   Write. Write a sentence about a TV show or movie you've watched recently. Use one word from **A** and one word from **B**.

_____

LANGUAGE FOCUS

A **Match the questions with the answers.**

1 You haven't been in a play before, have you? ○

2 The music was really loud, wasn't it? ○

3 This show is kind of boring, isn't it? ○

4 Matteo will be at the party, won't he? ○

5 You didn't enjoy the movie, did you? ○

○ **a** Yes, it is.

○ **b** No, I didn't.

○ **c** Yeah, it really was.

○ **d** Actually, I have.

○ **e** No, he won't.

B **Complete the tag questions with the appropriate words.**

1 The movie was really disappointing, _____?

2 You've never been to a movie studio, _____?

3 They can't go backstage without a pass, _____?

4 Jae-sun _____ seen the sequel yet, has he?

5 Kathy _____ buy our tickets for us, won't she?

C **Complete the conversation.** Circle the correct answers.

Marcy: That war movie was interesting. You enjoyed it, [1] **did / didn't** you?

Jesse: Oh, I loved it! I thought the acting was [2] **spectacular / overrated**. And the costumes were superb, [3] **were / weren't** they?

Marcy: Oh, yes. It must have taken a long time to make them.

Jesse: But I thought the plot was a bit [4] **unrealistic / gorgeous**. Most soldiers wouldn't do that in real life, [5] **would / wouldn't** they?

Marcy: Hmm … Probably not. Is there anything else you liked about the movie?

Jesse: I liked the [6] **music / special effects**. I'm definitely buying the soundtrack!

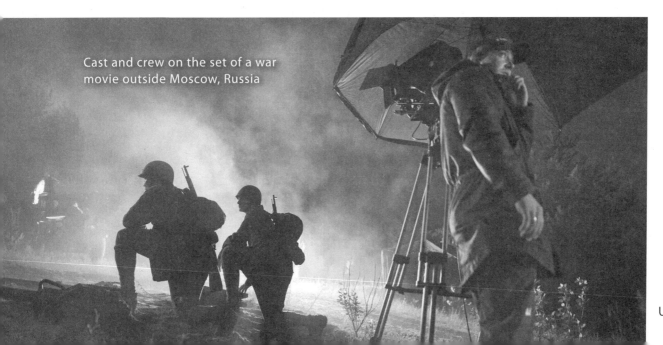

Cast and crew on the set of a war movie outside Moscow, Russia

THE REAL WORLD

MOVIE BUDGETS

A scene from the movie *Cats*

A **Scan the article.** How much money did the movie *Cats* bring in? _____

Movies are expensive to make. We often hear of movies with budgets of over a hundred million dollars. Some of these costs come from having a movie with famous actors or from filming in many locations. But there are also costs that people don't usually know about, such as the cost of music or the cost of providing food and drinks for the whole cast and crew. All these costs can add up to a huge amount of money in a movie's production budget.

But a movie's production budget doesn't tell the whole story. The marketing of a movie is very important, and movie companies sometimes spend large sums of money here. The 2019 film *Cats*, for example, had a production budget of $95 million, but marketing costs were an extra $100 million. Unfortunately, the film brought in only $75 million. It was a huge flop. Part of the reason for this was that *Cats* opened the same weekend as *Star Wars: The Rise of Skywalker*, which made over a billion dollars. However, it wasn't poor timing that ultimately doomed *Cats*. The movie received widespread criticism for having terrible special effects—something a $100 million marketing budget couldn't help.

B **Read the article.** Circle **T** for true or **F** for false.

1	A film's budget includes the cost of music.	T	F
2	The marketing of a movie can cost more than a film's production budget.	T	F
3	The main reason *Cats* flopped was because of poor timing.	T	F
4	*Cats* needed to make another $10 million to be considered profitable.	T	F

READING

A **Scan paragraph B.** Find and circle the name of a movie series that is also a video game.

ACTORS IN VIDEO GAMES

A Video games are a huge part of global culture today. In 2019, video gamers worldwide spent nearly $150 billion on video games. This is three times the amount the film industry earned in the same year. The game *Call of Duty: Modern Warfare* made over $600 million during its opening weekend in October 2019; very few movies have done that. To date, 2013's *Grand Theft Auto V* has sold 120 million copies, making over $7 billion. It's one of the best-selling entertainment products of all time. As games like these regularly make more money than Hollywood blockbusters, more and more movie stars are becoming involved in the video game industry in different ways.

A boxer wearing a special suit for recording motion capture

B One common way is for an actor to lend their voice to a video game character. Elijah Wood, who played Frodo in the *Lord of the Rings* movies, voiced the same character in the video game version of the series. Wood loved the challenge. "You find that the characters are in situations that are not real common and you have to … vocally make the character seem like he's going through some pretty intense situations," Wood said.

C Another way is to "act" in a video game. Through a technique called motion capture, game designers can create a character that looks and moves like an actual person. *Assassin's Creed* character Lucy Stillman was created based on the movements of actor Kristen Bell. Bell also lent her voice to the character in this popular series. Keanu Reeves plays the character Johnny Silverhand, a man with a robot arm, in the game *Cyberpunk 2077*.

D Movies and video games have become more closely aligned, and they share many similarities: complicated plots, unique characters, realistic acting, and thrilling action. The popularity of video games is likely to continue. So the next time you play a video game, keep an eye—or an ear—out for your favorite actor.

B **Answer the questions about *Actors in Video Games*.**

1 MAIN IDEA   What is the main idea of paragraph A?

   a   Some actors have found success in the video game industry.

   b   The video game industry is making a lot of money and is attracting more famous actors.

   c   Many actors prefer acting in video games than in movies because video games pay more.

2 DETAIL   How much money did video games bring in, in total, in 2019?

   a $600 million   b $7 billion   c $150 billion

3　INFERENCE　Wood thinks voicing a video game character is challenging because he has to _____.

　　a　use different accents　　b　read more lines　　c　react to unusual situations

4　DETAIL　Game designers use motion capture to create characters by recording a person's _____.

　　a　movements　　b　voice　　c　thoughts

5　VOCABULARY　The word *aligned* in paragraph D can be replaced with _____.

　　a　profitable　　b　connected　　c　respected

C　EXAM PRACTICE　Check (✓) the sentences the author would probably agree with.

a　☐　A video game made by a famous movie director is more likely to be successful.

b　☐　Many movie actors are doing voice acting to improve their acting skills.

c　☐　Video games will continue to be popular in the future.

d　☐　Most people in Hollywood don't respect actors who work in the video game industry.

e　☐　Working in the video game industry offers different challenges than working in the film industry.

VOCABULARY

A　**Complete the sentences.** Use the words in the box.

> appeal　　curious　　factors　　identify　　mood　　response

1　I'm _____ to know why you hate romantic comedies.

2　Actors who perform on stage receive immediate _____ to their work from a live audience.

3　My friends love horror films, but I don't understand their _____.

4　Filmmakers often use colors and lighting to set the _____ of a film.

5　That actor is easy to _____ because of his deep voice.

6　A good story is important, but there are many _____ that contribute to a great film.

B　**Write true sentences to help you remember these words.**

1　tension:　_____

2　horrible:　_____

3　unrealistic:　_____

4　gorgeous:　_____

5　overrated:　_____

WRITING

WRITING TIP USING DASHES, SEMICOLONS, AND COLONS

Be sure to use correct punctuation in your writing, including dashes (—), semicolons (**;**), and colons (**:**).

> - Use a **dash** to set off or emphasize information.
>
>   *The popularity of video games is likely to continue. So the next time you play a video game, keep an eye—or an ear—out for your favorite actor.*
>
> - Use a **semicolon** to separate two related sentences. Note the second sentence does not begin with a capital letter.
>
>   *The game* Call of Duty: Modern Warfare *made over $600 million during its opening weekend in October 2019; very few movies have done that.*
>
> - Use a **colon** to introduce a list.
>
>   *Movies and video games have become more closely aligned, and they share many similarities: complicated plots, unique characters, realistic acting, and thrilling action.*

A **Read the partial review of the video game _Spider-Man_.** Add a dash, semicolon, or colon to each blank (1–4).

Spider-Man is a well-known superhero [1] _____ he's also my personal favorite. In the video game *Spider-Man* (2018), Spider-Man must stop Mister Negative [2] _____ a superhuman crime lord [3] _____ from releasing a deadly virus in New York City. At the same time, Spider-Man has to deal with the personal problems of his civilian identity, Peter Parker. *Spider-Man* will appeal to anyone who enjoys a game full of action and surprises. Three things make this video game really good [4] _____ the story, the graphics, and the challenges. However, …

B **Choose a video game or TV show.** Take notes on it using the ideas in this chart.

Name	
Characters	
Plot/Story	
Who would enjoy it	
Things you like about it	
How it could be improved	
Overall rating (1–5)	

C **Use your notes from B to write a review of the video game or TV show.** Use correct punctuation.

10

I WISH
I COULD BE
AN OLYMPIC
ATHLETE!

A pole vaulter

PREVIEW

A Complete the wishes with the phrases in the box.

> could find a cure for cancer   were able to breathe underwater
>
> were an Olympic athlete   could make myself invisible

1 I wish I _____. I would love to be
    able to help save people's lives.

2 I wish I _____. I could make my
    country proud by winning a medal.

3 I wish I _____. I could listen in on
    other people's conversations without anyone seeing me.

4 I wish I _____. I would spend all
    day exploring the ocean floor.

B Complete the phrases. Circle the correct answers.

1 **design** / **solve** a building   4 **play** / **travel** back in time

2 **read** / **predict** the future   5 **set** / **fix** a world record

3 **cure** / **repair** a disease   6 **do** / **make** a wish

C Write. Complete the sentence below with a wish of your own.

I wish I _____.

LANGUAGE FOCUS

A Complete the conversations. Circle the correct answers.

1 **A:** Where would you go if you **could** / **would** fly anywhere?

   B: **I'll** / **I'd** fly to Egypt to see the pyramids.

2 **A:** I wish I **am** / **were** taller.

   B: Really? If I had one wish, I'd **want** / **wanted** to be able to see through walls.

3 **A:** If you **don't** / **didn't** ever have to take an exam again, how would you feel?

   B: **I'd be** / **I'm** thrilled!

B Correct the error in each question (1–5). Then match the questions with the answers (**a–e**).

1 If you are a time traveler, which time period would you go back to? _____

2 If you inventing a robot, what would it do? _____

3 If you could giving your mother any present, what would it be? _____

4 If you could be an architect or a lawyer, which will you be? _____

5 What do you wish you can do very well? _____

a An architect—I'd love to design interesting buildings for people to live in.

b I wish I could dance well. I'd like to be a professional dancer.

c I'd probably go back to ancient China.

d It would help doctors perform complicated surgery.

e I think some expensive jewelry would be the perfect gift.

C Complete the conversation. Put the sentences in the correct order (1–6).

a _____ Because some traditional languages are dying out. I'd like to help save them. It would be a shame if these languages disappeared completely.

b _____ Yes, it would, but flying's not really for me. I'm afraid of heights. I think I'd rather have the ability to speak every language.

c __1__ Hey, Lisa, if you could have a superpower, what would it be?

d _____ Let's see … If I could have any superpower, I'd want to be able to fly. That would be amazing, wouldn't it?

e _____ Every language in the world? Why?

f _____ That's true. Having that ability would also be great because you could easily speak to anyone you meet.

Finnegan tries on his Galacto costume.

A Skim the article. Choose the best title.

a Galacto Saves the City! **b** T-Storm Stops Galacto! **c** Who Is T-Storm?

The Make-A-Wish Foundation is a nonprofit organization that aims to improve the lives of children with life-threatening illnesses. It does this by granting wishes to sick children.

One child who was granted a wish was six-year-old Finnegan from Chicago. "Finnegan was very excited to talk about what he thought his wish might be," said Jessica Miller from Make-A-Wish. "He wanted to be a superhero, fight the bad guys, and break a brick wall. He did all of those things today." Finnegan chose the superhero name Galacto. He also chose his older brother Colman to be the bad guy, T-Storm. As the name suggests, T-Storm is able to control the weather.

Finnegan worked with the police to catch T-Storm. They received printed descriptions and photos of him. It wasn't long before they heard of a T-Storm sighting. After a helicopter search, they spotted him on a lake. They then took off on a high-speed boat ride. But T-Storm was not easy to catch. They chased him in a police car and even on foot before T-Storm was finally stopped.

The day ended with a news conference, where Galacto was thanked by the mayor for saving the city. It was a day Galacto—or Finnegan—will never forget.

B Read the article. Choose the correct answers.

1 What was Finnegan's wish?

   a to join the police force   **b** to be a superhero   **c** to fly a helicopter

2 Who chose Colman to be the bad guy?

   a Make-A-Wish   **b** the mayor   **c** Finnegan

3 Who can control the weather?

   a Galacto   **b** T-Storm   **c** both Galacto and T-Storm

4 What type of transportation did Galacto NOT use?

   a a plane   **b** a boat   **c** a car

READING

A Skim the article. What do the three people have in common? Check (✓).

a ☐ They each gave a speech at the UN.

b ☐ All of them have a disability.

c ☐ They are all actively involved in sports.

d ☐ They are all trying to make a difference.

Nickar Panyphorn addressing the UN

WORKING TOWARD CHANGE

In 2019, several young people captured the world's attention after giving speeches at the United Nations on World Children's Day. Among them were Jane Velkovski, Nickar Panyphorn, and Volodymyr Charushyn. All three
5 are working to improve the lives of children.

Jane Velkovski, North Macedonia

Jane, 11, cannot walk. He has a disease that requires him to use a wheelchair. However, this hasn't stopped him from doing what he wants. He is a strong supporter of children's rights, especially every child's right to participate in sports, no matter their disability. Jane plays
10 soccer whenever he can, and he is often the first person on the field. He has been active in several disability campaigns in North Macedonia, and is a frequent speaker at conferences.

Nickar Panyphorn, Laos

Nickar, 15, is an advocate for education in Laos. Her goal is to see every child attend school and receive a good education so they can reach their full potential. Nickar works with
15 her country's government to improve the education system and to promote children's participation in decision-making processes. She has met with children from various provinces across the country, and creates spaces where they can be heard and taken seriously. To Nickar, no child should be left behind.

Volodymyr Charushyn, Ukraine

20 Volodymyr, 16, had an accident when he was young that caused him to lose his ability to hear. For a long time, he felt very alone. He wished that he could communicate more easily with other children outside of his special school. As a result, he decided to promote the use of sign language in his hometown. He and his friends developed an interactive alphabet that uses hand movements and wooden cubes. He was able to place these cubes in public
25 places like playgrounds. Thanks to Volodymyr's efforts, hearing and non-hearing children can now communicate and play together in his hometown.

B Answer the questions about *Working Toward Change*.

1 `DETAIL` What is Jane's goal?

    a that every child be able to walk

    b that every disabled child receive a wheelchair

    c that every child be able to do sports

2 VOCABULARY Another word for *advocate* in line 13 is _____ .

    a teacher   **b** opponent   **c** supporter

3 PARAPHRASE What's another way of saying *no child should be left behind* (line 18)?

    a No child should develop faster than others.

    b No child should be ignored or forgotten.

    c No child should criticize their classmates.

4 CAUSE-EFFECT How did Volodymyr lose his hearing?

    a He had an accident.   **b** He had a disease.   **c** He was born that way.

5 DETAIL Who has a disability?

    a Jane and Nickar   **b** Nickar and Volodymyr   **c** Jane and Volodymyr

C **EXAM PRACTICE** **Match.** What did each person most likely say in their speech? One quote is extra.

1 Jane   ◯   ◯ **a** "Education is the mother of success. Today a reader, tomorrow a leader."

2 Nickar   ◯   ◯ **b** "In order to care for nature, we must know and learn about it."

3 Volodymyr ◯   ◯ **c** "My friends and I have long dreamed of breaking this barrier … between hearing and non-hearing people."

                           ◯ **d** "I don't let anyone joke about the issues I have with walking. I want to tell the whole world that everyone is equal."

VOCABULARY

A **Complete the sentences.** Use the words in the box.

> event   inspired   invention   pressure   reality   represent

1 The speech that she gave really _____ a lot of young people.

2 If we expect companies to change their environmental policies, we need to put _____ on them.

3 He has to face the sad _____ that he may never walk again.

4 The bake sale will be the school's main fundraising _____ this year.

5 This monument is meant to _____ famous political leaders from the past.

6 The world changed dramatically after the _____ of the phone.

B **Complete the sentences.** Circle the correct answers.

1 Wish me **luck** / **lucky** on my exam tomorrow.

2 If you see a shooting star, **make** / **take** a wish. It may come true!

3 Edward took part in the marathon **off** / **against** his doctor's wishes.

4 If you could **take** / **grant** anyone a wish, who would you choose?

5 It was his **dying** / **living** wish to see the Grand Canyon one more time.

WRITING

WRITING TIP **USING A VARIETY OF STRUCTURES**

Use sentences of different lengths, types, and structures to add variety to your writing.

> - Use sentences of different lengths.
>
>   *I closed my eyes tightly as I tossed the coin into the well, and then opened them to see if my wish had come true. It had.*
>
> - Use both active and passive sentences.
>
>   *I picked a tiny four-leaf clover from the field near my house. I've been told that a four-leaf clover brings good luck. I put it between the pages of my book.*
>
> - Vary your sentence openers.
>
>   *At 10 o'clock that night, my sister and I decided to go outside to look at the stars. Within minutes, we saw a shooting star.*

A **Read the partial paragraph below.** Highlight the longest and shortest sentences. Underline an example of the passive voice.

If I could change something about myself, I'd be a little taller. This would help me be a better basketball player. It might also help with my confidence. I also wish I could play the piano. In my opinion, the piano is one of the most expressive instruments. My brother and sister both play well, but for some reason, I was told by my parents that I should learn the trumpet. Unfortunately, I hated the trumpet! Of course, I gave it up quickly. For a third wish, I'd like to be able to paint well. I …

B **Look back at the partial paragraph in A.** Circle three different types of sentence openers.

C **Write a paragraph.** Describe three things you wish you could change about yourself. Give reasons or explanations for each wish. Use a variety of sentence structures.

11

WHAT WOULD YOU DO?

PREVIEW

A Complete the sentences. Use the words in the box.

> cheated   damaged   lied   lost   stole

1 Paula _____ to her parents about where she went last night.

2 Zac _____ on the test; he copied his classmate's answers.

3 Michi _____ her sunglasses. She might have left them on the bus.

4 Brandi just _____ a pack of gum. I saw her put it in her pocket.

5 Kyle borrowed his dad's car without permission and _____ it when he hit a trashcan.

B Match the situations (1–4) with the advice (a–d).

1 The diners at the table next to Juan are really noisy. _____

2 Lily borrowed your book but then lost it. _____

3 James cut in front of Beth when she was standing in line to get movie tickets. _____

4 Fareed found a wallet full of cash on the sidewalk. _____

a She should offer to replace it.

b He should take it to the police.

c She should tell him to wait in line like everyone else.

d He could say something to the manager.

C Write. Whose action in **A** do you think is the worst? Write what you think that person should do.

_____

LANGUAGE FOCUS

A **Complete the sentences.** Circle the correct answers.

1 You **should** / **shouldn't** talk in the library.

2 If a teacher accidentally **gave** / **would give** you an A+, what would you do?

3 My wallet **was stolen** / **has been stealing** from my backpack.

4 My homework isn't in my bag. I **should leave** / **must have left** it at home.

5 My neighbor **has been** / **could try** playing loud music every night recently.

6 Steve **must** / **couldn't** have broken the window. He wasn't there.

B **Complete the sentences.** Use the correct form of the verbs in parentheses.

1 What have you _____ (**do**) for the last 30 minutes?

2 My uncle _____ (**take**) to the hospital last night.

3 The children have _____ (**watch**) cartoons all day long.

4 This building _____ (**design**) by a famous architect in 2018.

5 These houses _____ (**paint**) last year.

6 I've _____ (**feel**) really tired lately.

C **Read the conversation and correct five errors.**

Wes: Hey! Where's my chocolate bar? It was here on my desk a few minutes ago, and now it's gone.

Maria: I have no idea. Maybe someone ate it. Anyone could have came in here and taken it from your desk.

Wes: Who would do that? I've been looked forward to eating it all day.

Maria: Well, you could asked the people in the hallway. Maybe someone will admit they took it.

Wes: I don't think so. If someone takes it, they probably wouldn't admit it.

Maria: Yeah, you're probably right. I think you would keep your food inside your backpack next time.

Wes: I'll definitely do that. Thanks.

THE REAL WORLD

A teenager is unsatisfied with her meal.

A Skim the article. Choose the best title.

a Is It OK to Lie?   b Lying Is Wrong   c The Truth Hurts

We all lie. Despite the fact that we've been taught that lying is wrong, everyone has lied at some point in their lives. But is lying really always wrong?

Consider this situation: You go to a friend's birthday party. The food her mother prepared doesn't taste good. If your friend's mother asks you if you enjoyed your meal, you don't want to offend her, so you say, "Yes, it was great, thanks." We call this a "white lie"—a lie that's seemingly innocent and does no harm.

Are there situations where lying is necessary? Imagine this: You're in a supermarket, and a frantic young man runs by you and hides in a corner. Seconds later, an angry-looking person with a knife comes in asking if you've seen a young man run past. What would you do? If you tell the truth, the young man may get hurt. Lying may in fact save his life.

On the other hand, consider the birthday party scenario again. Telling your friend's mother a lie will not help her improve her cooking. She's likely to serve the same bad food again in the future. So, the question remains: Is it OK to lie or not?

B Read the article. Choose the correct answers.

1 According to the article, lying is sometimes necessary in order to _____.

   a find out the truth   b save time   c prevent bad consequences

2 The word *frantic* in the third paragraph means _____.

   a very sad   b very anxious   c very tall

3 Which of these statements would the author most likely agree with?

   a People who often lie can't form good relationships with other people.

   b A lie can be bad or helpful depending on the situation.

   c Telling the truth is the best way to deal with any situation.

READING

A **Skim the article.** What could be another title for this article?

   a The End of Piracy   **b** Piracy—A Profitable Business   **c** The Problem of Online Piracy

THE HIDDEN COSTS OF ONLINE PIRACY

A Have you ever downloaded songs, TV shows, or movies from the internet without paying for them? Have you ever shared music, TV shows, or movies on an online file-sharing network without the owner's permission? If you have answered "yes" to either question, did you know that you're considered an online pirate?

B Nearly 190 billion visits were made to illegal piracy websites in 2018. Most people know that piracy is a crime—so why do they still do it? If you download a movie or song from a file-sharing network, it's free. And it's easy to do. Online piracy is quick, and the files are instantly available. And if nobody gets hurt, is it really a crime?

C In reality, piracy can cause serious harm to content owners—they don't receive any income from pirated goods. But the impact is wider than that. A recent study on music piracy reported that the damage to the industry results in more than 70,000 lost job opportunities and $2 billion in lost wages each year in the U.S. alone.

D At one point, it was thought that the trend of online streaming services such as Netflix would help reduce online piracy. However, this has not been the case. Today, users are likely to "streamrip," or illegally download files that are being played on streaming platforms. So while the legal streaming of content has grown, so has piracy.

E In addition, a new piracy market has emerged in recent years: books. The rise of ebooks has made the process of downloading and sharing books online much easier. Unfortunately, this form of piracy has discouraged well-known authors from writing more books, and has resulted in loss of employment for many people in the book publishing industry.

F Piracy is a serious problem in many countries, and many laws have been put in place to counter it. In the United States, offenders could be fined and even jailed. Other countries have their own laws against piracy. So the next time you're thinking of downloading something illegally, think of the people who will be affected by your actions. Don't be an online pirate!

B **Answer the questions about _The Hidden Costs of Online Piracy._**

  1 `INFERENCE` According to paragraph B, most people engage in online piracy because _____.

     a others are also doing it   **b** it's hard to detect   **c** it's convenient

  2 `DETAIL` Which of the following statements is NOT true?

     a Content owners receive more income from pirated goods.

     b Online piracy is quick, easy, and usually free.

     c Online piracy can lead to an increase in unemployment.

3 DETAIL According to the article, what did people think might help reduce online piracy?

    a educating people about why piracy is wrong

    b increasing the availability of online streaming services

    c making physical products cheaper and more accessible

4 PURPOSE What is the purpose of paragraph E?

    a to state the author's opinion

    b to describe a growing trend and its effects

    c to make a prediction about the future

5 INFERENCE Does the author feel that online piracy is a crime?

    a yes   **b** sometimes   **c** The author's position isn't clear.

C   **EXAM PRACTICE** **Complete the summary.** Use words from the article.

Online ¹ _____ is a global problem. Consumers know it's wrong, but they do it anyway, mostly because downloading and sharing files is fast and easy. People also believe piracy does not ² _____ anyone. However, piracy is a crime and can cause serious harm to the economy.

While it was believed that the increase in online streaming services like ³ _____ might reduce piracy, this has not happened. The more people stream, the more piracy has grown. Besides music, TV shows, and movies, the illegal downloading of ⁴ _____ has become a serious problem in recent years.

There are many laws in place that aim to fight piracy. In the United States, for example, online pirates could be ⁵ _____ ; some could even face jail time.

VOCABULARY

A **Complete the sentences.** Circle the correct answers.

  1 When you *blame* someone for a mistake, you think they **caused** / **corrected** it.

  2 If something *connects* two things, it **joins them** / **keeps them separate**.

  3 An example of a *crime* is **forgetting a friend's birthday** / **stealing money**.

  4 When something *splits*, it **forms one thing** / **divides into two or more things**.

  5 You might do an *experiment* to **relax after a long day** / **test if something is true**.

  6 If a person *robs* a bank, they **steal money from it** / **open a savings account**.

B **Read the sentences.** Choose the correct tense for each **bold** verb.

1 He **cut** the grass so it would look nice for the photos.   **a** present   **b** past

2 My feet **hurt**, so I think I'll take it easy today.   **a** present   **b** past

3 The two teams tied for first place, so they **split** the prize money.   **a** present   **b** past

4 The runner **quit** before finishing the race.   **a** present   **b** past

5 I always **put** salt on my tomatoes.   **a** present   **b** past

WRITING

WRITING TIP   **USING PERSUASIVE LANGUAGE**

Use persuasive language to make your opinion or argument stronger. Look at these phrases:

I strongly believe (that) …	*Clearly, / Obviously, / Surely, …*
Of course, …	*I'm sure/certain (that) …*
Without a doubt, …	*From my point of view, …*

A **Circle the choice that expresses your opinion.**

1 It's **sometimes** / **never** OK to look through someone's phone without their permission.

2 Stealing food is **acceptable** / **unacceptable even** if you are starving.

3 Playing video games is **good** / **bad** for kids' health and development.

4 There **should** / **shouldn't** be a minimum legal age for cell phone use.

B **Choose one statement from A.** List three reasons to support your opinion.

Reason 1	
Reason 2	
Reason 3	

C **Use your notes from B to write a paragraph expressing your opinion.** Use persuasive language to strengthen your argument.

> I strongly believe that there should be a minimum legal age for cell
>
> phone use. One reason is that …

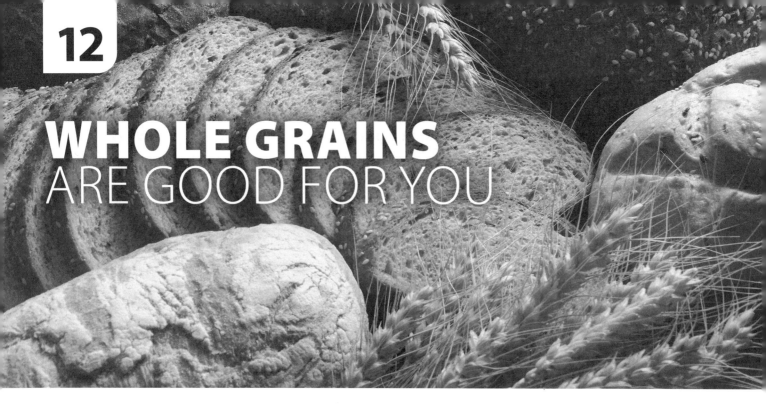

12

WHOLE GRAINS
ARE GOOD FOR YOU

PREVIEW

A **Complete the sentences.** Circle the correct answers.

1 Brown rice and oatmeal are examples of **red meat / whole grains**.

2 Meat, nuts, and tofu are good sources of **protein / salt**.

3 Too much **water / sugar** can cause weight problems and diabetes.

4 **Poultry / Healthy** fats like olive oil can be good for your heart.

B **Complete the sentences.** Use the words in the box. Two words are extra.

> exercise   limit   minerals   red   sugar   vegetarian   whole

1 It's best to _____ regularly to maintain a healthy body weight.

2 It's OK to eat _____ meat like beef and lamb, but eat it in moderation.

3 Eating less _____ can help you lose weight.

4 Some people think that a(n) _____ diet is healthier than a meat-based diet.

5 Fruits and vegetables contain a lot of important vitamins and _____.

C **Write.** Complete these sentences with your own ideas.

1 It's better to eat _____ than _____.

2 Too much _____ in your diet can be bad for you.

3 You should try to get at least _____ hours of sleep every night.

LANGUAGE FOCUS

A Complete the sentences. Circle the correct answers.

1 Whole grains are **as healthy** / **healthier** than processed grains.

2 This coffee is not **hot enough** / **hottest**.

3 Roberto likes **eat** / **eating** Italian food.

4 Yogurt, **which** / **who** has a lot of calcium, is good for you.

5 I think mental health is **most important** / **as important as** physical health.

B Correct the error in each sentence.

1 Eat less salt can lower your blood pressure.

2 Lean meat—like chicken and turkey—is healthier as red meat.

3 My sister Louisa is the fitter person I know.

4 The bakery is just around the corner, does it?

5 I'm not enough fit to run five kilometers.

6 My doctor, which helped me improve my diet, also suggested I join a gym.

C Match. Join the two parts of the conversation.

1 Hey, Matt, do you want to join me for a walk in the park? ○

2 You don't look so good. You didn't get much sleep last night, did you? ○

3 You know, playing video games is fine, but you should try and exercise more. ○

4 Well, have you ever tried indoor rock climbing at the mall? It's a fun way to get a full-body workout. ○

○ **a** No, I didn't. I was up all night playing video games with my brother.

○ **b** No, I haven't tried that, but that's a great idea. We can get lunch at the food court after—something healthy, of course!

○ **c** I'm sorry, Ari. I don't feel like going for a walk today. I'm too tired.

○ **d** You're right. You're fitter than me. What kind of exercise would you suggest?

A salad with grilled grasshoppers

THE REAL WORLD

DON'T LET INSECTS BUG YOU!

A Scan the article. Underline the four insects that are mentioned.

Don't be surprised to see a grasshopper on your plate in Denver, Colorado. More and more high-end restaurants in this American city are experimenting with edible insects on their menus.

Nearly all of Denver's edible insects come from the Rocky Mountain Micro Ranch, Colorado's first and only edible insect farm. It's located in a converted shipping container in southwest Denver. When founder Wendy Lu McGill opened the farm in 2015, she was shocked that they were the first in the market. "It was inconceivable to me that no one was doing this," she said.

Even in open-minded Denver, McGill knew she would face certain prejudices when it came to suggesting people eat more bugs: "There's an entire aisle in the grocery store selling things to kill the item I'm trying to get people to eat." Luckily, she says, insects are delicious. According to McGill, crickets taste like tofu. Ants have a lemony taste. Waxworms remind some diners of vanilla and honey.

Justin Cucci was the first chef in Denver to introduce insects at his restaurant. He's also one of the few chefs to have insects permanently on the menu. Like McGill, Cucci believes it is only a matter of time before we see more insects on the menus of restaurants in other American cities.

B Read the article. Circle **T** for true or **F** for false.

1 The Rocky Mountain Micro Ranch supplies most of Denver's edible insects.   **T   F**

2 When Wendy Lu McGill opened her farm, there were already a few others   **T   F**
   like it in the market.

3 McGill says that waxworms have a nutty taste similar to tofu.   **T   F**

4 You can always find a dish with insects in it at Justin Cucci's restaurant.   **T   F**

READING

A Skim the article. Add these headings (**a**–**d**) to the correct places.

a Use Your Senses　　**b** Visualize It　　**c** Classify Information　　**d** Use the First Letters

HOW TO IMPROVE YOUR MEMORY

The brain is not a computer. If it were, we'd never forget anything. But sometimes we do. Scientists believe that certain foods may boost memory, such as fatty fish, nuts, eggs, blueberries, and dark chocolate. Foods that are not good for the brain include sugary drinks and processed foods. Besides good nutrition, there are other tricks you can use to improve your memory.

1 _____ Your mind is like a filing system. You'll find it easier to remember information when it is grouped or organized. If you are going shopping, for example, organize your list in your mind— perhaps by grouping the meat, vegetables, and dairy items separately.

2 _____ Create a picture in your mind. This can help you remember something else. When you think of the image, you can think of the piece of information you assigned to it. For example, if you can't remember your student ID number—482310—try this: Maybe 48 is your house number, 23 was the jersey number of legendary basketball player Michael Jordan, and you have 10 toes. Picture yourself at your front door greeting Michael Jordan, but he steps on your 10 toes.

3 _____ You can stimulate more of your brain if you involve your other senses when trying to memorize information. When you activate more of your brain it may help you remember better. Writing out your notes while saying them aloud is one well-known study trick. Tapping your toes can help you remember songs.

4 _____ Acronyms and acrostics are shortcuts to remembering. An acronym is a word formed by the first letters of other words. The name "Roy G. Biv" helps you remember a rainbow's colors: red, orange, yellow, green, blue, indigo, and violet. Acrostics are similar to acronyms, but in a sentence. To remember the clockwise order on a compass, just think of "Never Eat Sour Watermelons" (north, east, south, west).

There are many other ways we can memorize information. By making our brain do these "mental workouts," we can make it better at storing and recalling information, and keep it healthy.

B Answer the questions about *How to Improve Your Memory.*

1 DETAIL What's good to eat or drink if you want to improve your memory?

　a a can of soda

　b a handful of blueberries

　c a frozen milk chocolate dessert

2 DETAIL What does the author say our brain is similar to?

   a a type of food   **b** a picture   **c** a filing system

3 VOCABULARY Which two words in tip 3 have similar meanings?

   a *stimulate* and *activate*   **b** *involve* and *memorize*   **c** *senses* and *songs*

4 INFERENCE What is true about acronyms and acrostics?

   a They involve multiple senses.

   b They are useful for people who cannot spell well.

   c They help us remember a list of words in the correct order.

5 COHESION Where is the best place for this sentence?

The more unique the image, the easier it will be to remember.

   a at the end of tip 1   **b** at the end of tip 2   **c** at the end of tip 3

C EXAM PRACTICE **Match each situation with the memorization method used.**

1 To remember a poem, Claudia sings it and acts it out in front of a mirror.   ○   ○ **a** visualization

2 To remember the order of the planets from the sun, Sam memorizes the sentence *My very educated mother just served us noodles.*   ○   ○ **b** an acrostic

3 To remember the conjunctions *for, and, nor, but, or, yet,* and *so,* Karima remembers the word *fanboys.*   ○   ○ **c** using the senses

4 To remember that the capital of Bulgaria is Sofia, Jay pictures a bull named Gary wearing a cap while sitting on a sofa.   ○   ○ **d** classification

5 To help her remember her errands, Carol divides them into things to do before lunch and things to do after lunch.   ○   ○ **e** an acronym

VOCABULARY

A Match the words with their definitions.

1 boost ○   ○ **a** to make something

2 calculate ○   ○ **b** an action or sound that gives information

3 produce ○   ○ **c** to improve or increase something

4 signal ○   ○ **d** to count the amount of something

5 solve ○   ○ **e** the place something comes from or starts at

6 source ○   ○ **f** to find an answer to a problem (e.g., how to reduce world hunger)

B **Complete the sentences.** Circle the correct answers.

1 Your five **senses / sensations** are the abilities of sight, smell, hearing, touch, and taste.

2 A **sensitive / sensational** event causes great excitement and interest.

3 Actions that are **sensible / sensational** are based on reason, not emotion.

4 A **sensor / sensation** is a physical feeling.

5 If you are **sensitive / sensory** to someone's feelings, you have a good understanding of them.

WRITING

WRITING TIP **USING SIMILES AND METAPHORS**

Use similes or metaphors in your writing to create a vivid image in the reader's mind. A simile compares things using *like* or *as*, whereas a metaphor says that one thing *is* something else.

Similes	Metaphors
*My best friend sings **like** an angel.*	*The classroom **was** a zoo.*
*The exam hall was **as** silent **as** the grave.*	*Life **is** a rollercoaster.*

A **Read the sentences below.** Circle **S** for simile or **M** for metaphor.

1 Time is money. S M

2 Celia couldn't believe her eyes—it was like a dream. S M

3 Mark's heart is made of stone. S M

4 Jack and Harry are twins, but they're as different as night and day. S M

B **Choose one of these topics and make notes about it.** Include at least three tips.

- how to get healthy, glowing skin
- how to keep your brain healthy
- how to keep your heart healthy
- how to achieve a healthy weight

Tip 1	
Tip 2	
Tip 3	

C **Write a paragraph using your notes from B.** Include a simile or metaphor.

It's easy to have healthy skin. If you follow these three tips, you will soon have skin as smooth as silk. First, eat a balanced diet. Eat a variety of fruits and vegetables, and avoid oily, processed foods. And of course, drink plenty of water to keep your skin hydrated. Second, …

LANGUAGE NOTES

UNIT 1 I LOVE MIXING MUSIC!

TALKING ABOUT HOBBIES AND INTERESTS (USING VERB + -ING)	
What are your hobbies? What do you **like doing** in your free time?	I **love reading** comic books and fantasy novels. I **enjoy doing** jigsaw puzzles.
Do you **like playing** chess?	Yes, I love it! Yes, I like it (a lot).
	I don't mind it.
	No, I don't like it (very much). No, I can't stand it.
Skiing is such good exercise!	**Gardening** is kind of boring.

UNIT 2 HOW LONG HAVE YOU BEEN DOING ARCHERY?

DESCRIBING ACTIONS THAT CONTINUE TO THE PRESENT (USING PRESENT PERFECT PROGRESSIVE)		
Sandra looks tired. She**'s been working** hard lately. Nick and Tina are in great shape. They**'ve been going** to the gym a lot recently.		
How long **have** you **been doing** archery?	I**'ve been doing** it	**for** a year. **since** last year.
What **have** you **been doing** all day?	I**'ve been watching** TV.	

UNIT 3 WHAT SHOULD I DO?

ASKING FOR AND GIVING ADVICE (USING MODALS)	
I left my phone on the bus. **What should I do?**	You **should call** the bus company.
	You **could call** your number.
I don't know what career to pursue. **What do you suggest I do?**	You **could try talking** to a guidance counselor.
	Why don't you do some online research?
I'm not doing very well in my algebra class.	**Have you thought about getting** a tutor?
I'd like to get a new phone, but I can't afford it.	**If I were you, I'd continue** using your current phone.

UNIT 4 THE KOALA WAS TAKEN TO A SHELTER

TALKING ABOUT THINGS THAT ARE/WERE DONE (USING PASSIVE VOICE)

The vet **wraps** the koala in a blanket.	→	The koala **is wrapped** in a blanket.
He **is washing** the baby rabbit carefully.	→	The baby rabbit **is being washed** carefully.
Someone **left** the dog at the shelter.	→	The dog **was left** at the shelter.
Was the dog **abandoned**?		Yes, it was. / No, it wasn't.
How often **are** the animals **fed**?		Every four hours. / Six times a day.

UNIT 5 HOW ARE THEY MADE?

TALKING ABOUT HOW THINGS ARE/WERE DONE (USING PASSIVE VOICE + BY)

A machine **cuts** the wood.	→	The wood **is cut by** a machine.
A factory worker **checks** the pencils.	→	The pencils **are checked by** a factory worker.
The customer **chose** the design.	→	The design **was chosen by** the customer.
A logging company **cut down** the trees.	→	The trees **were cut down by** a logging company.
The store **has customized** the shoes.	→	The shoes **have been customized by** the store.
The pencils **are made of** soft wood.		

UNIT 6 LOOK AT THOSE NARWHALS!

ADDING INFORMATION TO A SENTENCE (USING NON-DEFINING RELATIVE CLAUSES)

The narwhal, **which is a type of whale**, has a long tusk.

The dugong, **which is a kind of mammal**, is sometimes called a sea cow.

Last weekend we went to the aquarium, **which now has a collection of seahorses**.

My uncle, **who visits us every summer**, is a marine biologist.

My cousin Lisa, **who is a scuba diving instructor**, knows a lot about coral reefs.

If you have questions, ask the tour guide, **who is an expert on ocean conservation**.

UNIT 7 IT MIGHT HAVE BEEN A TEMPLE

DESCRIBING PROBABILITY (USING MODALS OF PROBABILITY)

	Less Sure	More Sure
Present	The lost treasure **could/might** be in a cave. But the treasure **might not** even exist.	The jewels **can't** be in that cave—it's too high. This gold necklace **must** be valuable. No one's ever found the treasure. It **must not** exist.
Past	This house **could/might** have belonged to the royal family. However, it **might not** have belonged to an important person.	The house is huge, so it **must** have belonged to the royal family. There are bedrooms in the building, so it **couldn't** have been a school.

UNIT 8 IT'S TALLER THAN THE EIFFEL TOWER!

DESCRIBING AND COMPARING THINGS (USING *TOO*, *ENOUGH*, COMPARATIVE/ SUPERLATIVE ADJECTIVES)

You can't get to Arsenalna Station on just one escalator. It's **too deep**.
Celia is **old enough** to drive. But Max is only 14, so he is**n't old enough** to drive.
Elevator 1 is just **as fast as** Elevator 2. But it's **not as large as** Elevator 2.
The new hotel is **taller than** the clock tower. It was **more expensive** to build **than** the mall.
The castle is **the oldest** building in the city. It's also **the most popular** tourist attraction.

UNIT 9 HE'S A GREAT ACTOR, ISN'T HE?

ASKING FOR CONFIRMATION OR INFORMATION (USING TAG QUESTIONS)

Leonardo DiCaprio **is** a good actor, **isn't he**?	Yes, he is.
That TV show **was** amazing, **wasn't it**?	Yes, it was.
You **liked** the ending of the movie, **didn't you**?	Yeah, I did.
You **haven't** been to the new movie theater, **have you**?	No, I haven't.
Meryl Streep **will** star in a new TV series next year, **won't she**?	Actually, she won't.
You **can't** see that movie until you're 18, **can you**?	No, I can't.

UNIT 10 I WISH I COULD BE AN OLYMPIC ATHLETE!

TALKING ABOUT WISHES AND IMAGINARY SITUATIONS (USING *WISH*, *WOULD* + VERB)	
I **wish** I	were famous. / **didn't have** so much homework. / **could play** an instrument.
If you **were** rich, **would** you **use** the money to travel?	Yes, I **would**. I**'d use** it to go to Antarctica.
	No, I **wouldn't**. I**'d donate** the money to charity.
If you **could have** any superpower, what **would** it **be**?	I**'d like** to be able to fly.
Where **would** you **go if** you **could go** anywhere in the world?	**If** I **could go** anywhere in the world, I**'d go** to Australia and New Zealand.

UNIT 11 WHAT WOULD YOU DO?

LANGUAGE REVIEW	
Present perfect progressive and passive form	**Describing probability**
She**'s been waiting** here for an hour.	You **must** be very relieved.
My neighbor **was taken** to the hospital.	This bag **could/might** belong to Ben.
Giving advice and talking about imaginary situations	That **can't** be her car. Hers is black.
	He **could/might** have taken the wallet.
You **should apologize** for saying that.	I **must** have left my homework at home.
If I **saw** a crime, I**'d call** the police.	She **couldn't** have left the book there.

UNIT 12 WHOLE GRAINS ARE GOOD FOR YOU

LANGUAGE REVIEW	
Gerunds	Tag questions
Exercising is a great way to relax.	Nuts **are** good for you, **aren't they**?
Describing and comparing things	Non-defining relative clauses
This banana is (**not**) **as ripe as** that one.	My aunt, **who studied medicine**, always gives good health advice.
I'm not going out today. I'm **too tired**.	Greek yogurt, **which has a lot of protein**, is good for you.
This coffee is (**not**) **sweet enough**.	

CREDITS

Photo Credits